Social Security Law in Finland

Social Security Law in Finland

Pentti Arajärvi

This book was originally published as a monograph in the International Encyclopaedia of Laws/Social Security Law.

Founding Editor: Roger Blanpain
General Editor: Frank Hendrickx
Volume Editor: Willy van Eeckhoutte

Wolters Kluwer

Published by:
Kluwer Law International B.V.
PO Box 316
2400 AH Alphen aan den Rijn
The Netherlands
E-mail: international-sales@wolterskluwer.com
Website: lrus.wolterskluwer.com

Sold and distributed in North, Central and South America by:
Wolters Kluwer Legal & Regulatory U.S.
7201 McKinney Circle
Frederick, MD 21704
United States of America
Email: customer.service@wolterskluwer.com

Sold and distributed in all other countries by:
Air Business Subscriptions
Rockwood House
Haywards Heath
West Sussex
RH16 3DH
United Kingdom
Email: international-customerservice@wolterskluwer.com

Printed on acid-free paper

ISBN 978-94-035-0543-5

e-Book: ISBN 978-94-035-0544-2
web-PDF: ISBN 978-94-035-0545-9

Printed in the United Kingdom.

The Author

Professor Pentti Arajärvi (born in 1948) studied at the University of Helsinki, Finland, and graduated in Law in 1972. In 2003, he defended his PhD dissertation on the justness of income security.

During his service at the Ministry of Education (1972–1984), his responsibilities included legislative preparation functions. Between 1984 and 2000 he was employed as a Committee Counsel by the Parliament of Finland and acted as the secretary for the Social Affairs and Health Committee and the Economic Committee. During these years, he also served as the political secretary of the Minister of Education and wrote a report on the reform of the Finnish income security. Thereafter, he was the leading researcher at the National Insurance Institution Kela (2000–2002).

From 2003 to 2011, he was Professor of Social and Education Law at the University of Eastern Finland and from 2011 to 2015 Professor of Social Law at the University of Helsinki.

Professor Arajärvi continues his work as an expert in social law and policy and constitutional law.

The Author

Table of Contents

The Author 3

List of Abbreviations 13

General Introduction 15

§1. General Background 15
- I. Country and Nation 15
- II. Judicial Conditions 17
- III. Economy 18
- IV. Labour Force and Employment 18
- V. Social Security 19

§2. Historical Background of Social Law 19
- I. Peasant State 19
- II. Autonomous Grand Duchy 20
- III. First Steps of Independent Finland 21
- IV. Constructions of the Welfare State 22
- V. New Economic Order 22
- VI. Nordic Model 23

§3. Sources of Social Security Law 24
- I. General 24
  - A. Social Welfare and Healthcare Services 24
  - B. Pecuniary Benefits 25
  - C. Scope of Persons Covered by Social Law 26
  - D. Operative Principles 27
- II. Legislation 27
  - A. General 27
  - B. List of Central Legislation 30
- III. Regulations 31
- IV. Adjudication 32
- V. Labour Agreements 32

Part I. Institutions 33

Chapter 1. Public Institutions 33

§1. Ministerial Departments 33

§2. PUBLIC INSTITUTIONS 33

Chapter 2. Position and Competence of the Public Institutions 35

Chapter 3. Private Institutions 36

Part II. Contribution and Financing 39

Chapter 1. Contribution Regulation for Employees 40

§1. FIELD OF APPLICATION 40
I. Territorial Field of Application 40
II. Personal Field of Application 41

§2. CALCULATION OF CONTRIBUTIONS 41
I. Calculation Base 41
II. Contribution Amount 42

§3. ADMINISTRATION 44

Chapter 2. Contributions for Public Sector Workers 45

Chapter 3. Contributions for the Self-employed 46

§1. FIELD OF APPLICATION 46
I. Territorial Field of Application 46
II. Personal Field of Application 46

§2. BASIS FOR CALCULATION OF CONTRIBUTIONS 46

§3. AMOUNT OF CONTRIBUTION 46

§4. ADMINISTRATION 47

Chapter 4. Other Contributions 48

Chapter 5. Government Funding 49

§1. FULL PAYMENT OUT OF GENERAL TAXATION 49

§2. RESIDUAL FUNDING 51

§3. EARMARKED TAXES 51

Part III. Healthcare 53

Chapter 1. General 53

§1. Territorial Field of Application 54

§2. Personal Field of Application 54

Chapter 2. Benefits 56

§1. Care Provided 56
I. Promotion and Protection of Health 57
II. Medical Care 60
III. Mental Healthcare Work 60
IV. Intoxicant Abuser Services 63
V. Rehabilitation 63
VI. Medical Use of Organs, Tissues and Cells 63
VII. Assisted Reproduction 64
VIII. Abortion 64
IX. Sterilisation 65
X. Pharmaceutical Service 65

§2. Amount of Benefit 65

§3. Determining Rates of Fees and Prices 67

Chapter 3. Conditions 71

Part IV. Family Allowances and Benefits 73

Chapter 1. Field of Application 73

§1. Territorial Field of Application 73

§2. Personal Field of Application 73
I. Maternity Package or Grant 73
II. Child Benefit 73
III. Child Maintenance Allowance 74
IV. Conscript's Allowance 74
V. Child Maintenance Credit 75
VI. Daily Childcare 75
VII. Support to Childcare 76

Chapter 2. Dependent Children 79

Chapter 3. Amount of the Benefit 80

Chapter 4. Payment 81

Part V. Incapacity to Work 83

Chapter 1. Field of Application 83

§1. Territorial Field of Application 83

§2. Personal Field of Application 83

Chapter 2. Benefits 84

§1. Funeral Benefit 84

§2. Incapacity to Work 84
I. Wage Earners 84
II. Self-employed 84
III. Other Persons 84

Chapter 3. Certification of Incapacity to Work 85

Chapter 4. Benefits 88

§1. Wage Earners 88

§2. Self-employed Workers 89

§3. Other Persons 89

Chapter 5. Conditions 91

Chapter 6. Accumulation Rules 94

Part VI. Industrial Accidents and Occupational Diseases 95

Chapter 1. Field of Application 96

§1. Territorial Field of Application 96

§2. Personal Field of Application 96

Chapter 2. Concept of 'Industrial Accident' 98

§1. Accident 98

§2. Link to the Contract of Employment 98

§3. Accidents on the Way to Work. 98

Chapter 3. Concept of 'Occupational Disease' 99

Chapter 4. Medical Care 100

Chapter 5. Incapacity to Work 101

Chapter 6. Death 103

Chapter 7. Prevention of Occupational Diseases 104

Chapter 8. Supplementary Benefits 105

Chapter 9. No-fault Insurance 106

Chapter 10. Civil Liability 107

Chapter 11. Accumulation Rules 108

Part VII. Unemployment Security and Employment Services 109

Chapter 1. Provision of Work 109

§1. Labour Meditation 109

§2. Vocational Training 111
I. General Vocational Training 111
II. Labour Training 111
III. Promotion of Employability 111
IV. Integration of Immigrants Through Employment 112

§3. Direct Work Provision 113

Chapter 2. Unemployment Benefit 115

§1. Field of Application 115
I. Territorial 115
II. Personal 116

§2. Amount of the Benefit 118

§3. Conditions 119

§4. Job Alternation Leave 121

Part VIII. Pensions 123

Chapter 1. Pensions for Wage Earners 125

§1. Old-age Pension 125
I. Beneficiaries 125
A. Territorial Field of Application 125
B. Personal Field of Application 125
II. Conditions 125
III. Pension calculation 129

§2. Survivors Pension 131
I. Beneficiaries 131
II. Conditions 131
III. Calculation 132

Chapter 2. Pensions for the Self-employed 133

§1. Old-age Pensions 133

§2. Survivors' Pension 134

Chapter 3. Disability Pensions 135

Chapter 4. Guaranteed Income for Old Persons 139

Part IX. People with a Handicap 143

Chapter 1. Social Integration 143

§1. General 143

§2. Special Services for Persons with Severe Disabilities 144

§3. Services for the Disabled Person under the Social Welfare Act 145

§4. Services for the Mentally Disabled Person 146

Chapter 2. Financial Allowances for the Handicapped 147

§1. Beneficiaries 147

§2. Conditions 147

§3. Benefits 148

Part X. Social Assistance 149

Chapter 1. Beneficiaries 149

Chapter 2. Conditions 150

Chapter 3. Amount of the Benefit 151

Chapter 4. Claims and Administration 153

Chapter 5. Reclaiming of Benefits Paid 154

Part XI. Claims and Adjudication 155

Chapter 1. Claims 155

§1. Introduction of Claims 155

§2. Protection Against Seizure and Transfer 157

§3. Legal Capacity to Receive Benefits 159

Chapter 2. Adjudication 160

Selected Bibliography 161

Index 163

List of Abbreviations

CoE	Council of Europe
EEA	European Economic Area
EFTA	European Free Trade Association
ILO	International Labour Organization
Kela	Kansaneläkelaitos (National Insurance Institution)
Keva	Public Pensions Institute
Mela	Maatalousyrittäjien eläkelaitos (Farmer's Social Insurance Institution)
NGO	nNon-governmental Organisation
OECD	Organisation for Economic Co-operation and Development
STUK	Säteilyturvakeskus (Radiation and Nuclear Safety Authority)
THL	Terveyden ja hyvinvoinnin laitos (Institute for Health and Welfare)
TVR	Työttömyysvakuutusrahasto (Unemployment Insurance Fund)
UN	United Nations
UNESCO	United Nations Educational, Scientific and Cultural Organization
Valvira	Sosiaali- ja terveysalan lupa- ja valvontavirasto (National Supervisory Authority for Welfare and Health)
WHO	World Health Organization
WTO	World Trade Organization

List of Abbreviations

General Introduction

§1. General Background

I. Country and Nation

1. Finland is located in the coniferous forest belt of Northern Europe, approximately between latitudes 60 and 70. The neighbouring countries are Sweden in the west, Norway in the north and Russia in the east. From the south to west, the country is surrounded by the Gulf of Finland, the northern part of the Baltic Sea and the Gulf of Ostrobothnia. Estonia lies 70 kilometres to the south on the other side of the Gulf of Finland. Correspondingly, Sweden is the neighbour across the Gulf of Ostrobothnia. About 10% of the country's surface is lakes and 70% forest.

2. Finland constituted the eastern part of the Swedish Kingdom until 1809. The west of Finland was annexed in the twelfth century. At the same time, Novgorod and later Russia expanded from the east to the west. In 1323, the Finnish eastern border was drawn for the first time. After this, the border moved first to the east and then returned westward, as Sweden started to lose its status as a great power.

3. After the war of 1808–1809 between Sweden and Russia, a sideline of the Napoleonic wars, Finland was annexed to the Russian Empire, with the status of an autonomous Grand Duchy. The Russian Tsar was also the Grand Duke of Finland. Throughout its autonomy, the country had its own administration, taxation right, civil service, Parliament and as of the mid-nineteenth century, its own currency. Finnish became the official language, side by side with Swedish, in the 1860s. The period of the Grand Duchy laid the foundations for the development of the country as a State. New and more versatile forms of business emerged and industrialisation took off. New industrial activities gave rise to the labour movement which was relatively reformist by nature and followed the German ideals to better the conditions of the labouring man.

4. What was problematic at the beginning of twentieth century was the contemporary Russification tendency prevailing in the Empire, resulting in the repeated disbanding of Parliament, used as the counterforce of the Russification policy. Legislative development came to an almost complete standstill. And finally, World War I closed almost all operations of Parliament. However, the Social Democrats gained a simple majority in the parliamentary elections of 1916. This Parliament enacted, among other legislation, an emergency powers act which, in practice, meant that Finland was virtually independent of Russia. The Act was never ratified and Russia's temporary government under Kerensky ordered new elections to be held in the autumn of 1917.

5. The new Parliament with a right-wing majority adopted the Acts on the eight-hour working day and unemployment funds. The question on the partitioning of land was taken into re-examination. However, consistent unrest followed in the country due to a bad crop, the end of the fortification work implemented by the Russians as a result of WWI, both contributing to the weakening of people's livelihood. Moreover, the March revolution in Russia had deprived the Empire of clear police authority.

6. In the situation generated by WWI and the Russian revolution, Finland was handed the opportunity to declare independence, and the resolution was passed in the Parliament on 6 December 1917. The above unrest led to a bloody civil war in the spring of 1918.

7. As agreed in the Molotov–Ribbentrop Pact, the Soviet Union attacked Finland towards the end of 1939. The Finnish Winter War lasted until March 1940. However, a new war broke between Finland and the Soviet Union in June 1941, lasting until 1944. The war continued in the northern part of the country until the spring of 1945 with the aim of expelling the German troops. In the peace treaty, Finland lost about 11% of its area and the second largest city Vyborg. The displaced population from the areas ceded to the Soviet Union were resettled in other parts of Finland. Finland retained its status as a Nordic parliamentary multiparty democracy.

8. In 2018, Finland has good 5.5 million inhabitants. The birth rate is about 1.65 children per woman. The ageing baby boomers of 1946–1950 cause a change in the demographics and, at the same time, the pensionable age goes up. The population numbers might start decreasing in a couple of decades but owing to immigration, the number keeps growing. The proportional share of the active working population is decreasing, causing the dependency ratio to weaken.

9. The Finnish population is quite homogeneous. Culturally, Finland belongs to the Nordic countries while the legal system is Germanic. The mainstream religion is the Evangelical-Lutheran faith (71%); the Orthodox account for about 1%, the other denominations for about 1.5% and the non-religious people for about 26% of the population.

10. Finland is a bilingual country, with Finnish and Swedish as the official languages. The Swedish-speaking population accounts for almost 7% of the population as do the speakers of languages other than these two national languages. The catering for the educational and societal needs of the Finnish- and Swedish-speaking populations is guaranteed on an equal basis through the Constitution. Moreover, the Constitution grants linguistic and cultural protection to the Sami (about 10,000) and the Roma (about 10,000) as well as to other minority groups.

II. Judicial Conditions

11. Until the declaration of Finland's independence, the Constitution passed on from the period of Swedish reign remained in force in the country. However, in 1906 the country was able to implement a parliamentary reform based on universal suffrage, and as a result, both women – first in Europe – and rest of the men, or about 80% with no vote so far, obtained the right to vote and stand for elections. In the first parliamentary election in 1907, already 19 of the 200 members of Parliament were women.

12. Enacted in 1919, the new Constitution guaranteed civil and political rights and regulated the competence of the major State bodies in accordance with the classic tripartite ideal. In 1995, the civil rights provisions of the Constitution were revised. They became modern basic rights, extended also to include economic, social and cultural rights as well as those related to the environment. The individual scope of these rights was extended to apply to any person covered by the jurisdiction of the country. In 1999, the Constitution and other constitutional laws were merged into one unified Constitution which entered into force on 1 March 2000.

13. Finland is a parliamentary democracy. The legislative powers are vested in Parliament, and the President plays a minor role in the sense that the laws are approved by the President who, on this occasion, can also return acts adopted by Parliament for a new reading. Amendments of the Constitution call for a qualified majority. Parliament is elected for a four-year mandate but upon the Prime Minister's proposal, the President can order new elections to be held already earlier. The President is elected by direct vote for a six-year term, and the elected President can be in office for two consecutive mandates. The executive powers are exercised by the government that must enjoy the confidence of Parliament. Parliament elects the Prime Minister, who is then appointed by the President, together with the cabinet proposed by the Prime Minister.

14. State regional government is organised into functional regions, and the south-west archipelago constitutes the autonomous Province of Åland. The autonomy of the Åland islands is underpinned by the guarantees given by the League of Nations in 1921. Åland has its own legislative body with limited law-issuing powers.

15. The local government unit is a municipality, and Finland's about 300 municipalities enjoy an autonomous administrative status. The number of municipalities is decreasing. Municipal self-government includes the right to organise the administration, levy taxes and decide on the municipal tasks – even though acts can be issued to impose new tasks on municipalities. Municipalities enjoy a strong status and in practice, they shoulder most of the welfare State tasks by law (social welfare and healthcare services, education).

16. Finland is a member of all major international and European organisations. The country joined the United Nations (UN) as anticipated as 1956, the same year in which it became a member of the Nordic Council. In 1995, Finland became a European Union country, having been a member of the European Economic Areas (EEA) since 1994. Moreover, Finland is a member of the Organisation for Economic Co-operation and Development (OECD), the Council of Europe (CoE) and various UN organisations (such as World Trade Organization (WTO), Word Health Organization (WHO), International Labour Organization (ILO) and United Nations Educational, Scientific and Cultural Organization (UNESCO)). Prior to becoming an EU State, Finland belonged to European Free Trade Association (EFTA).

17. As part of the above international co-operation, Finland is a signatory of all major UN and CoE human rights conventions. Through Finland's membership in the EU and EEA, the earlier extensive Nordic network of conventions is much reduced and is, in practice, today represented by the Nordic convention on social services.

III. Economy

18. In 1950, half of the Finnish population lived on agriculture and forestry. Most of the exports were constituted by forest industry products. As a result of the war repairs imposed on Finland, the metal industry and later also the clothing and chemical industries became the most important export industries, especially in the trade with the Soviet Union. From an agricultural society, Finland had a very rapid transformation into an industrial and service-based society. Looking at today's economic structure, 66% of the people are employed in services, a little less than 30% in industry and only about 4% in primary production.

19. Foreign trade has always played an important role in the Finnish economy. Finland's major export markets are Sweden, Germany and the United States and import markets are Sweden, Germany and Russia. Over 60% of all trading takes place with other EU countries.

20. In 2016, the annual income per wage earner was EUR 29,400.

IV. Labour Force and Employment

21. Traditionally, Finland's employment rate has been high, with the exception of the anticipated 1990s and the current financial crisis that started in 2008. In February 2018, the employment rate of men between 15 and 64 years of age was 70.5% while the corresponding percentage for women was 69. About 87% of the men and about 78% of the women had full-time employments. In February 2018, the unemployment rate was 8.6%, slightly higher among men.

22. Over 30% of the population over 15 years of age have a higher-level education while about 40% have a secondary schooling. The level of at least secondary schooling education is more than 80% among the population under 55 years. About 90% of employees are organised in unions or unemployment funds.

V. Social Security

23. The Finnish social security system is different from the insurance-based model prevailing in the European Union in the sense that the system is based on the place of residence. Finnish employee pensions, unemployment security, health insurance, parental insurance and accident insurance, including occupational diseases, are the most comprehensive systems underpinned by the social insurance. At the same time, however, the people residing in the country receive minimum benefits in the form of social allowance as well as the social welfare and health services organised by the municipalities. In healthcare services, the health insurance plays a minor role.

24. In Finland, the concept of 'social security' corresponds more or less to the term 'social protection' used in the EU contexts. The standard headings imposed on the text lead to a limited view of the Finnish social security system and its structure. Major parts of the service system are also left out, such as the housing and study support and several forms of social allowance. Benefits and services not based on the insurance system are mainly financed through taxes collected by the State and municipalities.

25. The structure of the social security system translates into the various functions of the benefits. The objective of the earnings-related and insurance-based benefits is to compensate for the loss of income when the respective risk materialises. Social allowances, which are quantified at a minimum level, are used to compensate for the living costs or to provide assistance in paying for them. Among the monetary benefits, the purpose of living assistance is to prevent want. The service systems meet needs irrespective of the insurance. The idea is to prevent social risks, to cover income deficiency to the extent that it is possible to do so through services, to maintain and promote people's functional capacity and subsistence as well as to create employability and schooling possibilities.

§2. Historical Background of Social Law

I. Peasant State

26. Organised social security dates back to the sixteenth century. King Gustavus Vasa (reigning from 1523 to 1560) and Gustav II Adolf (reigning 1611–1632) modernised the Swedish State, and the peasant farm became the economic base of the Kingdom. The farm provided livelihood to the people living on it while the Crown levied taxes and recruited soldiers. This structure was supported by the prohibition to partition land. The owner was responsible for the farm, for the people and for tax payments. The dwellers on the farm were subject to the farmer either as family members or on the basis of their hireling status.

27. From the seventeenth century, the livelihood based on the role of a hired employee, hireling, was gradually complemented by the almshouses and pauper care. Coming to the eighteenth century, the Kingdom of Sweden started to lose its status as a great power. The war with Russia in the early eighteenth century resulted in a population catastrophe further aggravated with years of famine.

Finland's population decreased from about 450,000 to 300,000. As a consequence of the depopulation, Finland suffered from lack of labour which led to the introduction of wages paid in money. Gradually, wages came to replace the hireling statuses, and the emerging industry, especially the manufactures, had a demand for paid labour. However, the real breakthrough of wage labour took place a century later.

28. The population catastrophe was also followed by a need to promote population growth, and as a consequence, the principle of not dividing the farms was abandoned and clearing of new fields was favoured. This situation led to the croft farming. The crofter was liable to pay rent in various forms of work. The number of independent farms increased. In terms of social policy, an important milestone was the introduction of pauper care as of the mid-eighteenth century. Under this system, the poor who were fit for work went around from farm to farm while those incapable were assigned, in a decreasing auction, to homes to be taken care of against a fee paid by the parish.

II. Autonomous Grand Duchy

29. A time of peace, fruitful for Finland, started in 1809 and brought about population growth. The partitioning of land remained a major social policy issue. The main solutions offered to the poverty problem were laws regulating pauper care and vagrancy. Every year, the landless people had to seek work from the farm owners of their municipality. The other option was to be declared vagrant. The army had been decommissioned, and therefore the consequence of vagrancy was either prison or expulsion to Siberia. Pauper care was targeted at poor children, the disabled persons and people who were too old to be able to work. The legislation was mitigated somewhat towards the mid-nineteenth century.

30. As of the 1860s, the need for industrial labour force started gradually to break down the local labour market, and the regulatory system focusing on social relations started to reform. The legislation on vagrancy became more controlling by nature, losing its labour policy character. The rise of the Finnish forest and paper industry played a significant role in the growth of industry as from the 1880s. The forests started to create value added which led to a firmer grip of the landowners on the use of the forests and taking of the timber by the landless population. Monetary economics grew in importance, and purchasing powers were concentrated in the landowners and town bourgeois classes. As a consequence of the social policy reforms undertaken in Germany under Bismarck and the increase of industrial wage-earning labour, Finland also introduced its first social insurance system through the enactment of the accident insurance legislation in 1895.

31. Agricultural labourers became employees at the service of industry. Use of child labour was restricted and both pauper care and vagrant legislation were reformed once again. Social security started to be characterised by the patriarchal attitude of the industrial tycoons and mansion owners. However, the founding of loan societies and granaries, instituted to prevent poverty and high mortality rates, played a more important role from a national and population perspective. The conditions of agriculture were also improved. Nevertheless, Finland remained one of Europe's most backward countries where infant mortality, for example, was almost 200 out of 1000 babies born.

III. First Steps of Independent Finland

32. The implementation of social security legislation was further postponed, including the introduction of the eight-hour working day. On the other hand, the pauper care act was reformed and the country enacted compulsory education laws. In the 1920s, new legislation was issued to safeguard the livelihood of single parents and orphans, marriage legislation was reformed and the country saw the founding of several civic societies focused on social issues. The Health Care Act was also reformed, together with the healthcare regulations to enhance preventive healthcare.

33. With the economic depression of the 1930s, unemployment soared to a record rate, causing the unemployment fund system to crash and be replaced by the institution of a new system. The depression of the 1930s also caused the organisation of public welfare to initiate: the decade saw the enactment of laws on child welfare, alcohol abuse and vagrancy. The first act on the statutory social insurance, the National Pensions Act, was adopted in 1937. The Act was based on individual insurance but in the legislative reform of the year 1957 social insurance was to become founded on a public system.

34. In connection to World War II, Finland fought the Finnish Winter War of 1939–1940 and the War of Continuation of 1941–1944 against the Soviet Union. To boost the war effort, the employer and labour organisations signed an agreement in 1940 on the negotiations on general working conditions, a breakthrough in the development of the collective agreement system. The post-war years saw the organisation of the care of invalids and war orphans, in particular. Free school meals had already become established during the war while the first general social policy legislation in the post-war years was the introduction of the child benefit system. The legislation of social assistance was also reformed.

IV. Constructions of the Welfare State

35. By Nordic standards, Finland started to build up the welfare State relatively late, in actual fact, only in the early 1960s. The prerequisites for the progress were the free trade arrangement with EFTA and the strongly developing trade with the Soviet Union. Legislative amendments were introduced at a brisk pace. The national pension system had already been reformed as of the year 1957, and the employee pension system came into being in 1962, the health insurance system in 1963 and the national survivors' pension system in 1968. Healthcare services were reformed through the Primary Health Care Act of 1972, children's day care through the legislation of 1973 while the education system reform took place in the turn of the 1960s and the 1970s. Other major reforms of the 1980s include the overall renewal of social welfare in 1982, the reform of the specialised medical care in 1989 and the complete reorganisation of unemployment security in 1984.

V. New Economic Order

36. The fall of the communist States of Eastern Europe and the end of cold war in the 1990s marked the advent of neoliberalistic thinking also in social policy. Towards the end of the 1980s, Finland – in unison with the other Nordic countries – deregulated its foreign currency policy, which resulted in a serious banking crisis and an economic depression. At the same time, the Soviet/Russian trade, vital for Finland, collapsed. In a few years, unemployment rates rose from 3% six-folding to 18%. The consequence of the depression was a decrease in several social benefits and the growing unemployment security expenditure put a significant strain on public economy. Municipalities made cuts in their service systems with the aim of making savings. Both the purchasing power of private households and the taxes collected by the State plummeted.

37. During this depression, the basic right provisions contained in the Constitution were amended as of the beginning of August 1995. In addition to the existing civil and political rights, people's economic, social and cultural rights became binding and obligatory. Moreover, the end of the cold war had made it possible for Finland to join the CoE in 1989 which meant that the country now faced an increased number of more specific human rights obligations. Although the direst economic slump had already been surpassed, the period was still characterised by widening income divides and growing inequality in unemployment, education, health and housing. Over-indebted households and so-called neo-poverty were the new phenomena of the era. On the other side of the society, partially as a result of fiscal policy, the country saw the emergence of a group living on capital income who, by converting their earned income into capital income with a lower tax rate, enjoyed a situation that was unparalleled.

38. Starting in 2008, the global financial crisis put an end to the relatively good growth of Finnish economy that had started after the depression in the 1990s. It has brought about lower employment rates and, despite a general economic growth, continued increase in inequality. The relative decrease in the public income has led to a permanent funding crisis faced by the social security system and the public economy at large, in turn leading to a situation where it is imperative for the country to impose radical reforms on its social welfare systems. When this book was being written, the pending reforms included the reorganisation of the administration and production of the social welfare and healthcare, the structural change of the system of municipalities and the respective legislative amendments. The recovery from the financial crisis seems to have started towards the end of 2017.

VI. Nordic Model

39. In the classifications of social security systems, Finland is grouped as part of the Nordic social security model. The Nordic model is characterised by its essential features which are generally thought to be universality, public service, high tax rates and a large share of public financing. The model is also partly underpinned by the high rate of organisation of employees.

40. Universality is a means to reach comprehensive social security. The basic idea is to provide the services to anyone residing in the country, irrespective of the labour market status or other socio-economic situation. Social welfare and healthcare services are also an indirect means of subsistence. If acquired privately, many services would probably be more expensive than they are when purchased with tax money.

41. The strong role of the government means that public authorities – in Finland mostly the municipalities – shoulder the responsibility for arranging the services and for the most part, also for providing them. In turn, the State has been responsible for the income protection systems. Combined with the universality of the system, this means that, for example, the services from services for handicapped persons to retirement homes are intended for anyone living in the country, not just for, for example, the low-income brackets, those with limited means or otherwise marginalised. This feature of the system is underlined by the so-called normality principle according to which also the special needs groups are taken care of, as far as possible, in the context of general services. The Constitutional Law Committee of Parliament has also highlighted the universality principle in its opinions by stating that the systems must not allow anyone to slip through the nets. This feature of the system is traditionally further enhanced by the extensive role played by different non-governmental organisations (NGOs).

42. Such a system calls for a high tax rate. This is made possible by the high rate of employment, underlined gender equality and active labour policy, the typical characteristics of the Nordic societies. This, in turn, is associated with the high rate of union membership and good collaboration between the social partners. The objective of relatively even distribution of income is also typical of these societies.

43. Over the past few years, the income divide has grown while the rate of organisation in unions and the rate of employment have somewhat decreased. The share of private social welfare and healthcare services has also grown although, for the main part, it is almost fully paid by the government.

44. The Nordic social security system is by no means a monolith. We could rather refer to five independent applications of Nordic social security, sharing certain features that distinguish them from other systems. Finland's unique character is particularly highlighted by its employee pension system which is based on private insurance. Other particularities include the lack of pension ceiling values and the status of the national pension in the pension system whole.

45. It is also typical of Finland that the minimum benefit system is more comprehensive than in other Nordic countries. For example, unemployment security is also granted to those who enter the labour market for the first time, and the parental allowance systems are, on a general level, more comprehensive than in the other Nordic countries. The benefits included in the Finnish income protection system are generally lower than in other Nordic countries but they are of longer duration and they are more inclusive in terms of accessibility.

§3. Sources of Social Security Law

I. General

A. Social Welfare and Healthcare Services

46. Originally, social welfare was created to improve the position of those in a problematic life situation. It was targeted, in particular, at the poor and the disabled persons or those otherwise in need of protection or care. The development of the social welfare State has changed the nature of the services that currently are often targeted at the whole general population. Today, the services are divided into general services and those specific to particular population groups. The general legislation covering social welfare services is the Social Welfare Act (1301/2014) that defines the social welfare field in its limited sense.

47. The special social welfare services are specifically targeted to children, the disabled persons and people with intoxicant abuse problems. Special services are regulated through particular legislation, such as the Child Welfare Act, the Services and Assistance for the Disabled Persons Act, the legislation on mental disability and the Act on Welfare Services of Intoxicant Abusers.

48. The legislative basis of healthcare is constituted by the Health Care Act, the Primary Health Care Act and the Act on Specialised Medical Care and the Mental Health Act. From the point of view of the patient, the core piece of legislation is the Act on the Status and Rights of Patients. In addition to it, healthcare is regulated through a copious number of other Acts and Decrees. Part of the legislation on healthcare also covers some aspects of social welfare, or vice versa; for example, intoxicant abuser services, old people's institutional care or mental health services are both healthcare and social welfare services.

49. An important part of healthcare services is constituted by the preventive services, including the health clinic services for infants and children under school age, the legislation on school and student healthcare services and occupational healthcare as well as the Health Protection Act that focuses on environmental healthcare. Other legislation with an impact on healthcare includes, among other, the acts on medical research, abortion, sterilisation and the medical use of human organs and tissues.

50. From a wider perspective, well-being is also promoted by legislation on housing production, labour policy and training as well as the various acts on educational and cultural services.

B. Pecuniary Benefits

51. The legislation regulating the arrangements for income support can be divided into four parts: (1) the income support system covering various risks comprising the earnings-related system to compensate for loss of income and the minimum security system that ensures basic subsistence; (2) the reimbursement of expenses; (3) the monetary benefits paid as an alternative for the provision of services; and (4) the social policy support provided through taxation.

52. The purpose of benefits based on earnings-related social insurance is to compensate for the non-obtained earnings. The systems are based on the insurance premiums linked to earnings and paid by the employer or the employee, in which case the level of the benefits is to a certain extent dependent on the quantity of the premium payments. The major systems are the employee pensions, the earnings-related unemployment benefit, the earnings-related sickness and parental allowance under the health insurance, the rehabilitation allowance and the benefits under the accident insurance. To a certain extent, earnings-related benefits are also paid to those participating in training.

53. The social allowance is a guarantee or support for basic subsistence. Often, the social allowances are of fixed quantity, paid through tax money and sometimes means-tested. Social allowances are normally paid on the same grounds as the earnings-related benefits. The particular characteristic of social allowances is their universality, meaning that they are applicable to anyone residing in the country. A particular form of social allowances is the social assistance, which is the last resort, means-tested system for basic subsistence. The purpose of this form is to cover the final cracks when, in the alternative, the person would slip outside all other forms of protection or be left at an insufficient level of subsistence.

54. The core of the systems is the compensations paid to families with children and the disabled persons, those to lower housing costs as well as the support granted to reimburse costs of illness, childbirth and rehabilitation. The particular significance of the cost compensations is the fact that they mostly lower the cost of living. In this way, they promote equality by offsetting the income divide between families with and without children, the disabled and not disabled persons, those with excessive and reasonable housing costs and the sick and those in good health.

55. In Finland, there are certain situations where support can be granted for those who take care of their situation autonomously, instead of providing them with the service. The major systems in this respect include the child home care allowance which replaces the day-care services as well as the family carer and caregiver supplements in situations where the alternative could be care in institutions. Often, these models are associated with partial support through the service system.

56. Finland applies some tax exemptions and deductions of social policy nature. The exemptions are generally associated with the compensations for costs. The deductions play a minor role; in practice, the national pension is free of tax and in State and municipal taxation, the lowest income brackets are eligible for a basic allowance. Certain tax exemptions and deductions are also associated with disability, maintenance liability and studying. The idea behind the small number of tax deductions is the fact that only taxpayers are eligible for them. For this reason, it is more rational from the social policy point of view to grant support instead of tax exemptions or deductions.

C. Scope of Persons Covered by Social Law

57. The Finnish social security system is based on universality which means that it aims at a coverage where nobody is discriminated against and that both the services and income protection comprise as widely as possible, i.e., in full all the people living permanently in Finland. Moreover, social security caters to the position of immigrants, especially asylum seekers. EU legislation often extends the benefits, especially those based on insurance, to the entire EEA area while there are also certain Nordic conventions that ensure services to those living in the Nordic countries.

58. Because of the residence basis of the social security system, it is necessary to define what residing in Finland means. In practice, this takes place through the Act on the Application of Residence-Based Social Security Legislation. The Act defines the coverage of the residence-based social security legislation, the impacts of entry and exit from Finland as well as the factors used to determine a person's ties to Finland. If necessary, an explicit decision will be made whether or not the Finnish social security legislation is applicable to a person. An appeal can be lodged against the decision.

59. In Finland, the social benefits and services are, as a rule, focused on the individual. The individual focus also applies to the criteria for granting the benefits, their level, the way in which the applications become pending and the implementation of the respective decisions. The individual nature of the criteria means that only the respective person's own income, assets, payments made by the individual, or other factors have a bearing on the granting and quantity of the benefit. The main exceptions to this principle are always based on the nature of the benefit. For example, it is not rational to grant housing allowance to entities other than families. Correspondingly, similar exceptions are applied to certain other benefits. On a general level, however, benefits cannot be granted, for example to the spouse or child of the insured, with the exception of the survivors' pension. In the same manner, the services are individualised even though the support measures can be targeted at the entire family. This is the case, for example, in child welfare.

D. *Operative Principles*

60. The municipalities are responsible for the organising and producing of services. In practice, the production of services of the smallest municipalities takes place at municipal federations, i.e. local government regional authorities. The State plays only a minor role in the production of services but it will participate in the respective financing. The services can also be produced by private actors in which case they are based on a contract between the municipality or municipal federation and the private service producer. In practice, they are purchased services that are mostly also subject to competitive tendering procedures.

61. The responsibility of the municipality or federation of municipalities is based on the home municipality system. Anyone permanently residing in the country is recorded as a member of a municipality, and as a result, the municipality in question is responsible for the individual's services. An exception is constituted by certain urgent measures taken in social welfare and healthcare, in which case temporary residence in a municipality is the basis for providing the service. In certain cases the person can decide which municipality's services they will use.

II. Legislation

A. *General*

62. Since 1995, the Finnish Constitution also contains specific provisions on social basic rights. They are focused on either the individual's rights or the duties of the public authorities. In the Finnish system, these basic rights are seen to constitute a direct liability of the authorities, and in particular cases, also as rules that generate rights to the individual. In certain senses, the basic rights also impact the relationships between private individuals.

63. The authorities are deemed to be liable for respecting, protecting and implementing the basic rights. The obligation of respect also includes the liability of government not to violate the basic rights. In turn, the obligation to protect makes the authorities liable to act if a third party violates the basic rights. Finally, the obligation to implement, which often relates to social rights but also to other rights, obliges public authorities to build up the infrastructure necessary for the materialisation of the right, and also see to the possibilities of practical operations.

64. The basic rights also have various impacts. Some of them constitute rights of individuals and others issue an assignment to the authorities while a part is relatively programmatic by nature. In addition, the basic rights play a role as the interpretation criteria for the application of law as well as factors that both limit the operations and generate possibilities for it.

65. In terms of social rights, section 19 of the Constitution is crucial. According to subsection 1, 'those who cannot obtain the means necessary for a life of dignity have the right to receive indispensable subsistence and care'. This provision is deemed to be in force as a subjective right and therefore, the government must, in these situations, secure the indispensable subsistence and care, in other words, the monetary benefits and services. Similar provisions are also contained, for example, in the Convention on the Economic, Social and Cultural Rights, the renewed European Social Charter and the Charter of Fundamental Rights of the European Union.

66. Under section 19, subsection 2 of the Constitution of Finland, public authorities must guarantee by law basic subsistence in the event of unemployment, illness and disability and during old age as well as at the birth of a child or the loss of a provider. The respective normal legislation is contained in the Unemployment Allowances Act, Health Insurance Act and the pension legislation.

67. In turn, section 19, subsection 3 decrees that the public authorities must guarantee adequate social welfare and healthcare services for everyone. Consequently, the public authorities must ensure that everyone has comprehensive access to the services in substance and geographically. The public authorities can meet this obligation through proper action or they can transfer it to NGOs or companies. The provision does not secure any explicit way of providing the services. The critical point in the provision is associated with the concept of 'adequacy'. It has been defined so that the services must provide every person with the conditions to act as a full member of the society.

68. The subsection 3 of section 19 also requires that the public authorities promote people's health. Here, we are faced with a shared right which calls for action by the public authorities, for example in arranging for the societal and health conditions.

69. Further in section 19, subsection 3, support is required for persons who are responsible for the development and upbringing of children. This provision is closely associated with the international Convention on the Rights of the Child which, among other stipulations, requires that societies must use their resources to improve the situation of children. This means material, intellectual and social support for the well-being of children.

70. Section 19 also requires that the public authorities promote the right of everyone to housing and the opportunity to arrange their own housing. The provision can be implemented through monetary benefits but also by means of housing production and similar actions.

71. Section 18 of the Constitution also has a social policy dimension because it, on the one hand, refers to everyone's right to earn their livelihood by the employment, occupation, or commercial activity of their choice, while it, and on the other hand, requires that the public authorities promote employment and work towards guaranteeing the right to work for everyone.

72. In section 16, the principle of basic education free of charge is complemented by the requirement that public authorities guarantee everyone equal opportunities to receive as well other education without being prevented by economic hardship. This provision is interpreted as containing the obligation to provide study support both in the form of lower study costs and living support during the studies.

73. In addition to the basic rights mentioned above, the provisions on equality, non-discrimination, linguistic and cultural rights as well as legal protection and good governance contribute to the implementation of social rights.

74. As a member of the European Union, Finland follows the Union law. The country is also a signatory of several human rights conventions containing social law provisions.

75. The Constitution provides for the conditions in which a public administrative function can be assigned to non-authorities. There are three such conditions. First, there must be an act that gives title to this; second, the transfer of the function must be necessary in view of the rational implementation of the function; and finally, basic rights, legal protection, or good governance must not be jeopardised. A function containing a significant use of public powers can only be given to the authorities. Significant use of public power is normally defined so that it entails the possibility to use measures against the interested person's will.

76. The organisation of Finnish social security is greatly influenced by the self-government of municipal residents. This self-rule covers, for example, the right of the municipality to levy taxes, to organise its own administration and to decide on the tasks and finances. However, tasks can be delegated to municipalities through specific acts. In practice, the social welfare and healthcare functions are widely delegated to the municipalities. The State must, however, ensure that the municipalities have the resources to enforce and implement such tasks. In practice, this takes place through the system of State subsidies allocated to municipalities.

B. List of Central Legislation

77. The following is a collection of the core legislation covering the Finnish social security system. These laws have been enacted by Parliament; under the Finnish Constitution, any individual rights and obligations, among other issues, must be based on formulated laws.

78. The list starts with certain acts with a wider perspective on social security. They do not fit into a list with sectorial categories. The funding-related laws cannot be classified under one title, either because part of this regulation is contained in the substantive laws while there is also specific legislation on funding.

General

Act on the Application of Residence-Based Social Security Legislation, 30 December 1993/1573
Act on Central Government Transfers to Basic Municipal Services, 29 December 2009/1704
Act on the Planning of and State Subsidies to Social Welfare and Health Care, 3 August 1992/733
Act on Customer Payments in Social Welfare and Health Care, 3 August 1992/734

Social insurance and assistance legislation

Unemployment Allowances Act, 30 December 2002/1290
Act on the Financing of the Unemployment Benefits, 24 July 1998/555
Health Insurance Act, 21 December 2004/1224
Act on Employers' Social Security Contribution, 4 July 1963/366

Legislation on accidents and occupational diseases

Occupational Accidents, Injuries and Diseases Act, 24 February 2015/459
Act on Compensation for Injuries or Diseases Originating during Studies in Circumstances Comparable to Work, 24 April 2015/460
Act on Compensation for Military Injuries and Diseases caused by the Service, 29 December 2016/1521

Legislation on pensions

Employees Pensions Act, 19 May 2006/395
Self-Employed Persons Pensions Act, 22 December 2006/1272
Farmers Pensions Act, 22 December 2006/1280
Seamen's Pensions Act, 22 December 2006/1290
Public Sector Pensions Act, 29 January 2016/82
National Pensions Act, 11 May 2007/568
Act on Guarantee Pension, 20 August 2010/703

Legislation on healthcare

Act on the Status and Rights of Patients, 17.8.1992/785
Health Care Act, 30 December 2010/1326.

Act on Specialised Medical Care, 1 December 1989/1062
Act on Private Health Care, 9 February 1990/152
Occupational Health Care Act, 21 December 2001/1383
Health Protection Act, 19 August 1994/763
Mental Health Act, 14 December 1990/1116
Communicable Diseases Act, 25 July 1986/583
Medicines Act, 10 July 1987/395
Act on Health Care Professionals, 28 June 1994/559

Legislation on social welfare

Act on the Status and Rights of Social Welfare Customers, 22 September 2000/812
Social Welfare Act, 30 December 2014/1031
Act on Private Social Welfare Services, 22 July 2011/922
Early Childhood Education Act, 19 January 1973/36
Act on Children's Home-Care and Private Care Allowance, 20 December 1996/1128
Family Allowances Act, 21 August 1992/796
Maternity Grant Act, 28 May 1993/477
Child Maintenance Act, 29 August 2008/580
Child Welfare Act, 13 August 2007/417
Conscript's Allowance Act, 20 August 1993/781
Act on Supporting the Functional Capacity of the Older Population and on Social and Health Services for Older Persons, 28 December 2012/980
Services and Assistance for the Disabled Act, 3 April 1987/380
Act on Interpretation Services for the Disabled, 19 February 2010/133
Act on Invalidity Benefits, 11 May 2007/570
Act on Special Care for Mentally Disabled Persons, 23 June 1977/519
Act on Family Caretaker Support, 2 December 2005/937
Family Carer Act, 3 April 1992/312
Act on Social Welfare for Intoxicant Abusers, 17 January 1986/41
Act on Social Assistance, 30 December 1997/1412
Act on the Professional Qualification Requirements of Social Welfare Personnel, 29 April 2005/272

Employment

Act on Public Employment and Business Service, 28 December 2012/916
Act on Rehabilitative Work Activities, 2 March 2001/189
Act on Integration of Immigrants, 30 December 2010/1386

III. Regulations

79. The regulation on social security is based on legislation. Under section 80 of the Constitution, 'the principles governing the rights and obligations of private individuals and the other matters that under this Constitution are of a legislative nature shall be governed by Acts'. This limits the importance of regulation that is of lower status than a law enacted by Parliament.

80. The Social Insurance Institution Kela has its own internal regulations related to the handling of benefits and legislative interpretations. However, they only apply to Kela's own operations and have no binding status, for example, in courts of law. Correspondingly, municipalities have their own ordinances to organise the municipal operations which are in line with the municipal autonomy principle.

IV. Adjudication

81. Court proceedings related to social security issues are mainly the competence of Administrative Courts and the Supreme Administrative Court. Legal disputes on income security are mainly subjected to the relevant complaints boards and, in the last resort, to the Insurance Court. However, the rulings by the superior Administrative Courts do not constitute precedents although, in practice, the rulings by the Supreme Administrative Court obtain this status. Court rulings are published at www.finlex.fi

V. Labour Agreements

82. Collective agreements have only minor importance in terms of social rights. In certain cases, they may extend legislative rights. Collaborating with government, the social partners participate in the legislative amendment preparations related to work-related benefits. The major areas include employee pensions and unemployment benefits which, in practice, are also funded by the parties in question. The legislation is always issued by the Parliament.

Part I. Institutions

Chapter 1. Public Institutions

§1. Ministerial Departments

83. At the general government level, the social security operations are under the umbrella of the Ministry of Social Affairs and Health. The Ministry's responsibility fields include promoting health and functional capacity, prevention of diseases, social welfare and prevention of social problems, social welfare and healthcare services as well as State subsidy issues, occupational healthcare, health protection, income security and the issues related to the National Insurance Institution (Kela). A minor part of social policy issues, such as the study subsidies, is organised under the auspices of the Ministry of Education and Culture. Moreover, the public sector pension schemes are administered by the Ministry of Finance.

84. Legislative preparation and State budget drafting are done by Ministries which also manage international affairs.

§2. Public Institutions

85. The following are organised under the Ministry of Social Affairs and Health: the Regional State Administrative Agencies for social welfare and healthcare and labour protection administration, the National Supervisory Authority for Welfare and Health (Valvira), the Radiation and Nuclear Safety Authority (STUK), the Institute for Health and Welfare (THL) as well as the Finnish Institute of Occupational Health and Kela. The appellate bodies or Appeal Boards organised under the Ministry of Social Affairs and Health are not, as such, courts of law but nevertheless regarded as judicial bodies.

86. The Insurance Court is the competent court for income security complaints. Organised under the Ministry of Justice, the Administrative Courts are the venues for the complaints concerning the services provided by the municipalities. The State Treasury which administers State pensions and Public Pensions Institute (Keva) is in charge of municipal, government, Church and pension schemes of Kela's personnel.

87. Organised under the Bank of Finland, the Financial Supervisory Authority also oversees social insurance matters.

88. The municipalities are in charge of the task of implementing almost all social welfare and health services. As Finnish municipalities enjoy a relatively extensive right of self-government, it will remain up to the municipalities themselves to determine how they organise the decision-making and modes of operation in this sense, as long as certain statutory minimum criteria are met.

Chapter 2. Position and Competence of the Public Institutions

89. Among the institutions and authorities under the Ministry of Social Affairs and Health, some are expert organisations that produce research data while others are regulatory and supervisory authorities.

90. In issues related to social welfare and healthcare services, the government officials have fairly limited competence and scope of operation because the responsibility for the services is almost entirely shouldered by the municipalities. The competence of government officials encompasses mainly State funding and service system supervisory issues. Appellate authorities are government bodies.

91. In terms of pecuniary income security, government administration is fragmented and mostly implemented through indirect public administration. In income security, the largest government authority is the Social Insurance Institution Kela which implements almost all legislation on social allowance and also manages the public health insurance and rehabilitation service. The major benefits managed by Kela include the pensions and related benefits under the National Pensions Act, the health and parental insurance, Kela's rehabilitation benefits, disability allowances, the basic unemployment allowance and labour market support under the unemployment security, certain family policy benefits and housing allowances. The Kela is supervised by a group of Trustees appointed by the Parliament.

92. On the general level, the social welfare services are operated by municipalities and listed in the Social Welfare Act, with the relevant tasks specified in special enactments. The most important among them are the Child Welfare Act, the Services and Assistance for the Disabled Persons Act, and on the health service side, the Health Care Act.

93. In implementing its tasks, the municipality will follow the general statutory modes of operation set for municipal operations, complemented by their own rules and regulations. Such rules and regulations contain more detailed guidelines covering the distribution of tasks and competence as well as the decision-making process of municipal organs and institutions.

94. The municipality bears the general responsibility for its inhabitants, i.e. persons with a domicile within the municipality. As concerns the social welfare and healthcare services, this illustrates the universality principle typical of the Nordic, and thus also Finnish, social welfare systems. In certain situations the municipality is also responsible for the care of persons who do not have their official domicile in the municipality. In these cases, it is normally a question of urgent needs of care or subsistence.

95. The operations of the municipalities are supervised by government authorities, and among them, the most important are the Valvira, the STUK and the Regional State Administrative Agencies, the latter mostly as the recipient of complaints.

Chapter 3. Private Institutions

96. Under the Finnish Constitution, 'A public administrative task may be delegated to others than public authorities only by an Act or by virtue of an Act, if this is necessary for the appropriate performance of the task and if basic rights and liberties, legal remedies and other requirements of good governance are not endangered. However, a task involving significant exercise of public powers can only be delegated to public authorities'. Normally, 'significant exercise of public powers' is understood as the independent discretion in the use of coercive measures or another significant interference with individual basic rights. Therefore, involuntary measures imposed on individuals, for example, cannot normally be delegated.

97. The most important measures of delegation within the service system include outsourced service purchases or the use of service vouchers. In the purchased service regime, the municipality directs the service user to a private service provider. In these situations, the legislation applicable to the services, the payments charged for them and the appellate system are the same as in the services provided by the municipality. This also applies to the quality requirements covering the care or treatment and to the other organisation of the operations. In the service voucher model, the municipality issues vouchers to the service user or patient, and they will autonomously seek the private service provider's services. The individual can use the whole sum of the voucher to cover the costs, and any remaining part of the sum is paid by the service user. In this model, the user enters into a contract under private law, and therefore the legal protection means and similar measures are based on consumer protection procedures. The third major system of supporting the operation of private service providers is constituted by the reimbursements payable under the Health Insurance Act for doctors' fees and examination and therapy costs. In these cases, the Social Insurance Institution Kela reimburses a predefined share of the service price directly to the service provider or to the user.

98. The private services are supervised by the municipality and regulatory authorities. The healthcare services and 24/7 social welfare services are subject to a permit issued by government authorities, while for the other services, the service provider must issue a notification on its operations.

99. The operations by private institutions account for a considerable share of Finnish income security. Here, the largest role is played by the employee pension institutions managing the private sector pension schemes. They are mutual companies, limited liability companies, funds or co-operative funds by legal form. Employee pension institutions underwrite pension insurance policies in line with the Employees Pensions Act and the Self-Employed Persons Pensions Act. The employer selects the employee pension institution which is, in turn, obligated to grant the private sector pension insurance as per the act in question. Company pension funds are institutions established by the employer, and there are also industry-wide pension funds.

100. Pension security is also provided by separately established private pension institutions that carry out a public task: Keva which is responsible for public pension insurance, the Farmer's Social Insurance Institution (Mela) and the Seamen's Pensions Fund.

101. The Finnish Centre for Pensions was founded for the management of the private sector pension systems but today, the public pension systems are also represented. The Finnish Centre for Pensions has certain tasks of public administration nature but its main responsibilities are related to the international administration of the pension system and to statistics, research, co-operation between the institutions and register maintenance as well as information and advice duties. The employee pension system is supervised by a government body, the Financial Supervisory Authority.

102. The accident insurance system is administered by private accident insurance institutions and, for the farmers, the Farmers' Social Insurance Institution. These institutions are responsible for the administration of the statutory accident insurance. As far as their insurance operations are concerned, they are supervised by the Financial Supervisory Authority.

103. The earnings-related daily allowances for unemployment are administered by unemployment funds. Most of them operate in association with the trade unions. The self-employed persons' unemployment funds and certain unemployment funds that also provide insurance to employees are separate institutions. An important actor for the financing of the unemployment insurance, the Unemployment Insurance Fund (TVR), also provides funding to the Education Fund, the wage protection system and employee pensions in cases where the pension is based on a period of unemployment. The insurance operations of these actors are also monitored by the Financial Supervisory Authority.

104. All private institutions involved in the provision of income security require a licence issued by the government. The financing of all institutions, also as regards their operating expenses, is based on parafiscal charges.

Part II. Contribution and Financing

105. Social security is financed through three different sources. The major element of service financing is taxation which means inflow of financing from both the State and the municipalities. The earnings-related income security is financed almost entirely through the salary, wage and earnings-based payments made by the employers and employees or self-employed persons. Minimum security is mainly financed with tax money. Certain services are also subject to user fees.

Chapter 1. Contribution Regulation for Employees

106. The employer is obliged to acquire employee pension insurance and pay the respective premium. The employer is free to choose the insurer which can be an employee pension company, or an industry-wide or company-specific fund. The Finnish Centre for Pensions monitors the fulfilment of these employer obligations. If no insurance is taken, the Finnish Centre for Pensions first invites the employer to rectify the neglect and can also take out the insurance at the employer's expense.

107. The unemployment security funding has three elements. The social allowance-based basic unemployment allowances and labour market supports are paid from State funds whereas the unemployment insurance payment collected from non-organised employees is used for the funding of the basic unemployment allowance.

108. Unemployment insurance premiums are not only used to finance the unemployment allowances but also certain costs incurred for training and job alternation compensations. The unemployment insurance is also used to fund pensions accumulated during the unemployment security periods (*see* paragraph 123).

109. The health insurance is composed of two different types of insurance, and the funding is likewise divided into the sickness benefits insurance and the earnings security insurance. The sickness benefits insurance covers medical expense reimbursements (medicines' reimbursements, rehabilitation services, reimbursements for doctor's fees, examinations, therapies and travelling expenses).

110. The earnings security insurance is used to fund the sickness benefits, the parenthood benefits and the rehabilitation benefits as well as occupational healthcare expenses. The earnings security insurance is fully paid for by the beneficiaries, employers, employees and self-employed persons. The premium contribution is determined on an annual basis. However, the State pays for the minimum-amount allowances payable for persons with no or minimal income.

§1. Field of Application

I. Territorial Field of Application

111. All employees in the private sector must be insured, also paying the employee pension premium on their work performed in Finland. Moreover, insurance must be taken on their work abroad as prescribed by international conventions and the EU legislation.

112. Unemployment security covers the permanent residents in Finland as well as those living abroad as defined by international conventions.

113. Everyone residing permanently is covered by the health insurance, as well as those living abroad covered by international conventions.

II. Personal Field of Application

114. All private sector employees must be insured for their work, and the employee pension premium must be paid starting from the month following their 18th birthday until the month in which they are 68. Seafarers and athletes constitute an exception with their own systems. The Seamen's Pension Act is applied to employees who perform work under the Seafarers' Employment Contracts Act on a Finnish vessel, and in certain cases, also on a foreign vessel. The athlete insurance relates to situations where the athlete receives a certain minimum pay for the sports activities.

115. The employee can take out voluntary insurance from an unemployment fund against unemployment. Moreover, all those residing permanently in Finland (*see* paragraphs 57–59) also have the right to receive unemployment benefits (*see* paragraphs 448–451 and 471–484).

116. The sickness benefits insurance under the health insurance covers all permanent residents of Finland, irrespective of their age, employment or other factors. The earnings security insurance under the health insurance covers all employees and self-employed persons residing permanently in Finland.

§2. Calculation of Contributions

I. Calculation Base

117. The basic pension under the Employees Pensions Act is fully covered by the premiums payable by the employers and employees.

118. The premium for the insurance under the Employees Pensions Act is determined on the basis of work-related earnings. The premium is paid on the basis of the work-related earnings accruing the pension. Another main principle is that the premium is based in the pay and other considerations agreed as the compensation for work performed. Normally, these items are also the same as the employee's taxable income. Certain company benefits and employment-based option arrangements constitute exceptions. Correspondingly, the basis of the premium payable by the employer for the employee pension insurance is constituted by the work-related earnings accruing the pension.

119. The employee is required to pay the annually adopted percentage-based unemployment insurance premium to finance the unemployment security scheme. In addition to the statutory unemployment insurance premium, the employees also pay a membership fee for their unemployment funds. Correspondingly, the employers pay an unemployment insurance premium adopted annually and based on the total wages and salaries paid. If a person works for a company in which he or she is one of the owners, the respective premiums will be adopted separately.

120. The premium payable by the insured for the sickness benefits insurance included in the health insurance is based on the taxable income determined for municipal taxation. The employer's premium for the earnings security insurance is the total of the pay. Both the employee and employer premiums are based on the taxable income in municipal taxation.

II. Contribution Amount

121. The employer's share of the employees' pension insurance premium varies according to the insurance: Is the insurance underwritten by an employee pension insurance company or a respective fund or foundation? In addition, the premium is dependent on the annual total number of work-related earnings paid each year, on the age and gender of the employees, amount of earlier invalidity pensions and unemployment pensions. The premium sum will be adopted on an annual basis.

122. As concerns the premium payable by the employee for the employee pension insurance, the share is set at a certain level so that there would not be a difference between employees in various sectors. However, the premium is higher for those between 53 and 62 years of age but they also accumulate the pensions at a higher rate in percentage.

123. Since pension is also accumulating during the periods of earnings-related unemployment benefit, the corresponding share is funded through unemployment insurance premiums. The TVR, which collects the premiums, will transfer a corresponding share to the Finnish Centre for Pensions, to be further distributed to pension institutes.

124. For historical reasons, the funding for the seamen's pensions follows a different system. The funding is divided so that the wage earner pays the same shares as any other employee while the employers contribute 13.2% of the total wages. The State covers a determined share of the pension expenditure.

125. The unemployment premium payable by the employees is the same for all whereas the employee's share of the premium varies according to the total of wages and salaries paid.

126. The employee's and self-employed person's shares for the premium of the care insurance under the health insurance and the earnings security insurance are determined annually. Likewise, the employer's share of the earnings security insurance premium is set annually. The funding of the sickness benefits insurance is divided in half between the insured and the State. The earnings security insurance is financed through premiums paid by the employees, employers and the self-employed while the minimum benefits are funded by the State.

Social Insurance Premiums, in Percentage of the Pay

Employers	*2018*
National Health Insurance	
– all employers	0.86
Unemployment insurance	
– total wages and salaries in 2018 less than EUR 2,083,500	0.65
– in excess of 2,083,500	2.60
– employer's unemployment insurance premium payable by co-owner	0.65
Employee pension insurance	
– Average employee insurance premium payable by the employer under the respective Act (Employees' Pensions Act)	17.75
– Average premium payable by the municipal employers (excluding the pension expenditure-based payment) (Public Sector Pensions Act)	17.75
– Average premium payable by government as the employer (Public Sector Pensions Act)	16.88
The Insured	*2018*
National Health Insurance	
Medical expenses premium	
– employees and self-employed	0.00
– beneficiaries (pension and benefit income)	1.53
Per diem premium	
– employees and entrepreneurs under the Farmers' Pensions Act	1.53
– Entrepreneurs under the Self-Employed Persons' Pensions Act	1.70
Unemployment insurance	1.9
– Premium payable by the co-owner/employee of the company	0.92
Employee pension insurance	
– employees under 53 years of age	6.35
– employees 53–62 years of age	7.8

– employees over 62 years of age	6.35
– the self-employed and farmers under 53 years of age	24.1
– the self-employed and farmers 53–62 years of age	25.6
– the self-employed and farmers over 62 years of age	24.1

§3. ADMINISTRATION

127. The employer pays their own share of the premium but also the contribution for the premium withheld from the employee, transferring the total to the pension insurance institution. Part of the pension funding under the Employees Pensions Act must be transferred to funds. Most of the accumulated premiums are spent in pension out-payments but a part is transferred to funds in view of future pension while one part is used for administrative expenses. The pension system gains proceeds from investment returns. Today, the Finnish pension funds amount to about EUR 199 billion.

128. The employer withholds the premium contribution and unemployment fund fees from the employees, transferring them together with the employer premium to the TVR. The fund also receives returns on its investments as well as certain other employer payments. The TVR pays a contribution to unemployment funds to be used for the earnings-related element of the unemployment security. In addition to their statutory contribution to the unemployment insurance premium, employees pay membership fees to their unemployment fund and this money also passes through the employer and the TVR. However, tax money is used to cover the share of the earnings-related unemployment allowance that corresponds to the basic allowance level.

129. The State collects her own and municipal taxes and transfers them to the *fiscus*.

Chapter 2. Contributions for Public Sector Workers

130. The holders of office and employees covered by the public sector (State, municipal and Church as well as Kela) pension systems pay the same employee pension premium as the employees on the private sector (*see* paragraph 126). The same way as in the private sector, the share payable by the public sector employers of the employee pension premiums is determined annually.

131. The municipal pension system provides for the future pension expenses by accruing funds, which increases the premium payable by the employer. In principle, this is also a system based on division but in practice, there are substantial funds accumulated in view of the future. The Church pension system operates in the same manner.

132. The State pension system is also a division-based system in principle, but also the State has a pension fund which is used to offset the cost burden of future pensions. Every year, about 40% of the State pensions are paid from the fund while the rest comes from the State budget allocations.

133. The employees in the public sector are treated in the same manner as the private sector employees (*see* paragraph 126) as far as the unemployment insurance premium is concerned. With the exception of the State, the employer is covered by the same premium payment obligation as the private employers.

134. The same applies to the health insurance.

Chapter 3. Contributions for the Self-employed

§1. Field of Application

I. Territorial Field of Application

135. *See* 126.

II. Personal Field of Application

136. *See* 126.

§2. Basis for Calculation of Contributions

137. Upon the entry into force of the pension insurance of the self-employed person, an annual work-related earnings sum is determined, constituting the basis for later payments and the accumulation of the pension. The earnings, i.e. the reported income corresponds to the pay that should reasonably be paid to a person hired to perform the same tasks or the remuneration that would otherwise be seen to correspond to the work in question. The same reported income is also used as the basis for the health insurance and parental insurance. It also is the basis for unemployment security if the self-employed person has taken a corresponding insurance policy. The reported income can be changed if there has been a major change in the circumstances. The amount is not tied to the result of the company.

138. In case of farmers, the earnings are defined on the basis of the income from the arable land while the forestry income is determined on the basis of forest surface. There are separate provisions for the income of one and two self-employed persons. Also fishermen and reindeer herders are covered by their particular provisions. The Farmers' Pensions Act is also the legislative basis for the pension for receivers of grants and scholarships. The calculation basis is the amount of the grant.

§3. Amount of Contribution

139. The financing under the Self-employed Persons Pensions Act is based on a division system. The self-employed pays an annual premium corresponding to the pensions for a year. Mostly, the premium income is not fully sufficient, and the part missing is paid out of State funds. The funding of the farmers' pension system is not sufficient to cover the annual out-payments of pensions and so as high a share as 70% of these pensions are covered by State tax money.

140. The self-employed person starting the business will be awarded a 22% reduction of the premium payment for the forty-eight first months of operations. It will also be possible to apply for flexible payments for one calendar year at the time. The number of such flexible-payment years is limited to the maximum of three during a period of seven years, if the payment is reduced. There are also upper and lower limits imposed on the reduced premium.

§4. Administration

141. Self-employed persons pay their pension premiums directly to the pension insurance institute. Farmers and recipients of grants pay their pension contributions to the Farmers' Pension Fund.

142. The self-employed persons and farmers who choose to take out insurance against unemployment pay the respective premiums to an unemployment fund.

143. The health insurance payment is collected together with the taxes in the same manner as the employee contributions.

Chapter 4. Other Contributions

144. The funding of the accident insurance, which also covers occupational diseases, as well as other accident-related insurance policies is based on normal insurance procedures. The policyholder is the employer or other party carrying the risk. In the accident insurance, the employer's responsibility is based, in principle, on the liability for damages, but it also covers occupational diseases and accidents taking place during commuting. Correspondingly, the insurance company's liability to indemnify covers the damages caused. The employer is obligated to take out insurance. The premium is determined on the basis of actuarial criteria.

Chapter 5. Government Funding

§1. Full Payment out of General Taxation

145. Both social welfare and healthcare services are mainly financed with tax money. The relatively few services organised by the State are normally fully paid with State taxes. Employment services constitute one example.

146. Most of the social welfare and healthcare services are maintained by municipalities, and the taxes collected by municipalities are used for their financing but the State also contributes through the central government transfers to municipalities. An important principle governing this system is that the central government allocations or transfers must allow every municipality to produce the necessary services. This is underpinned by the constitutional self-government of the municipal inhabitants, and part of that is the economic and operative capacity of the municipalities. As the State has transferred tasks to the municipalities, the State must also guarantee that the municipalities have the necessary operative conditions.

147. There are significant differences in the central government transfers to municipalities allocated to cover operating expenses on the one hand and founding costs on the other hand. The central government transfers to cover operating expenses are based primarily on the Act on the Central Government Transfers to Basic Municipal Services whereas the legislation applied to founding costs are the Act on the Planning of Social Welfare and Health Care and Central Government Transfer and the Act on Discretionary Government Transfers.

148. The Act on the Central Government Transfers to Basic Municipal Services is applied to almost all social welfare and healthcare services organised by the municipality. These are statutory tasks imposed on the municipality. The central government transfers allocated for the financing of basic services are divided into five parts or components. The general component is constituted by the so-called basic price which is augmented by a certain increase element, and this sum is multiplied by the number of inhabitants in the municipality. The increase elements applicable to the general component are related to aspects such as the location of the municipality in the archipelago, in remote areas, the municipality's population centre structure, language structure and change in its inhabitant numbers. The second component of the central government transfer is constituted by the calculatory costs of social welfare and healthcare while the third criteria is mainly based on education costs, the fourth on culture costs and the fifth on the costs incurred because of sparse population.

149. The calculatory costs for social welfare and healthcare are obtained by adding up all calculatory costs of the municipality, constituted by elements such as its age structure, rate of unemployment and need for child welfare services. The healthcare costs per age groups as well as morbidity rates are also taken into account. This calculation is further revised with the factor reflecting sparse population, and finally, the overall calculatory costs are determined on the basis of the municipality's number of inhabitants.

150. The situation of municipalities vis-à-vis each other is equalised on the basis of their tax income. The principle is the following: the municipal income is compared to the average income of all municipalities, and the difference in terms of a determined percentage value of the average is added to the transfer allocated to the municipality. However, municipal tax income in excess of a determined sum will decrease the central government transfers to it. This is the way to take the differences in municipal assets into consideration. Discretionary criteria are also available.

151. The system is extremely complex as it is designed to account for the differing conditions of the municipalities, particularly their geographic inconveniences and language situations. Moreover, below-average municipal tax proceeds, unemployment rates and morbidity and ageing of the population are taken into consideration in allocating the central government transfers to cover the operating costs of municipalities.

152. When the annual government transfers are being determined, the expected changes in the scope and quality of the associated municipal tasks as well as in the cost levels are also considered. The past year's materialised cost level is also taken into account. A nationwide adjustment is performed every four years. Based on the results, the municipalities are assigned their respective percentages of central government transfers as well as their rate of self-financing. Self-financing covers about two-thirds of the municipal costs.

153. Central government transfers to founding costs are granted to implement the national development programme if and when the State budget envisages appropriations destined for this purpose. Central government transfers can also be granted for founding projects which are indispensable for securing the social welfare and healthcare services of an individual municipality or a local government regional authority or to implement a project under the development programme. The transfer amounts to 25%–50% of the confirmed costs.

154. Social allowances are financed with tax money. Every year, the State allocates financing to the Kela for the benefits that are not based on insurance or financed by other parties. In practice, the Social Insurance Institution is in charge of all social allowances. The only insurance-based benefit system administered by Kela is the health and parental insurance.

155. The TVR makes an annual transfer from the accrued unemployment insurance premiums paid by the employees to Kela, with the sum corresponding to that collected from employees not belonging to unemployment fund. This results from the fact that the payment is statutory and obligatory but taking out insurance is voluntary for the individual. Other exceptions include the financing of the home care allowance for children by the municipalities because this form of benefit and care is an alternative to the day care for which the municipalities are responsible. Moreover, to activate the employment obligations imposed on municipalities, there are provisions requiring the municipalities to finance certain allowances related to long-term unemployment.

156. Municipal pensions are covered in line with the division system principles so that the employee contributions are complemented with municipal taxes in accordance with annually adopted payment rates. Moreover, the municipal system envisages reserved accumulated in view of future pensions. Likewise, the State pensions follow the division system and are funded, in addition to the employee contribution, through State taxes.

157. The State tax financing covers the element of all pensions not based on employment. These include the pensions accumulated during child care and study.

158. The national basic unemployment allowance, labour market support and the basic element of the earnings-related daily allowance are funded with State tax money. The basic allowance is also funded through the employees' unemployment insurance premiums (*See* paragraph 107) while the earnings part of the earnings-related allowance is funded through the unemployment insurance contributions made by the employees and the employers (*See* paragraph 119).

159. The State pays half of the health insurance-related sickness insurance contribution out of the tax revenues. Moreover, the State pays the minimum allowance element of the health insurance-related earnings security insurance, in other words the costs incurred for the sickness and parental indemnities paid to those not employed.

§2. Residual Funding

160. The funding of the self-employed persons' and farmers' pensions, based on their contributions, is not enough to cover the pension expenditure. The State covers the rest through tax money (*See* paragraph 139). Likewise, the State pays a part of seamen's pensions.

§3. Earmarked Taxes

161. According to Finnish legislation, all social insurance contributions are taxes to be used for a certain purpose.

Part III. Healthcare

Chapter 1. General

162. The Finnish healthcare system comprises healthcare which means maintenance, promotion and protection of health, as well as medical care and medical rehabilitation. Normally, these are activities carried out by healthcare professionals.

163. The core of the healthcare system is constituted by the services provided by the public sector, mainly municipalities. The municipalities are liable to take care of everybody residing in their territory. They can organise care on their own, collaborate with other municipalities or use the local government regional authorities for the purpose. Municipalities can also contract third-sector organisations or companies to provide the care, or they can use so-called service vouchers. In addition, the health insurance system provides support to the insured who use private healthcare services. Anyone residing permanently in Finland is insured.

164. The purpose of healthcare is to promote and maintain public health, well-being, working and functional capacities as well as social security. Other objectives include the aim to bridge the health differences between different population groups as well as to guarantee equal access to services, their good quality and patient safety.

165. Oral healthcare services comprise the promotion and follow-up of health, health consultation and check-ups, examination, prevention and treatment of oral diseases, early identification of particular support and examination needs of patients, as well as referring the patient, if necessary, to further examinations and treatments.

166. The basic legislation in healthcare is the Health Care Act which contains provisions on the municipalities' responsibility for the promotion of health and well-being, basic healthcare and specialised medical care.

167. Organised by the municipality, primary healthcare comprises the follow-up of public health, promotion of health and the inherent health consultation and check-ups, oral healthcare, medical rehabilitation, occupational healthcare, environmental healthcare, accidents and emergency services, outpatient care, home nursing, hospital-at-home services, hospital care as well as mental healthcare and intoxicant abuser work to the extent that they do not fall within social welfare or specialised medical care services. Specialised medical care includes the prevention of diseases classified according to the specialities in medicine and dentistry as well as the healthcare services related to the respective examination, treatment, emergency care, on-call duty and medical rehabilitation. Specialised medical care can also be provided in the form of special-level treatment in the case of rare or particularly demanding specialised medical care tasks.

168. Promotion of health refers to the operations targeted at the individual, population, communities or living environment, with the objective of both maintaining and improving people's health and working and functional capacities and impacting on the factors underpinning health. In the promotion of health and well-being, the objective is to exercise influence not only by using conventional healthcare methods but to also through every other aspect of municipal activities, from housing to environmental protection. The municipalities are obliged to give an annual well-being report to the municipal council.

169. Every municipality must belong to a hospital district which will have a healthcare organisation plan drafted. The plan contains an agreement on the co-operation of municipalities, the objectives and responsibilities in the promotion of health and well-being, the organisation of healthcare services as well as the way in which the specialised medical care functions are attended to.

§1. Territorial Field of Application

170. The healthcare system comprises the territory of the Republic of Finland as well as other healthcare based on international conventions.

§2. Personal Field of Application

171. The healthcare system covers all persons residing permanently in the country, and in emergencies also any other individual. The patient access to treatment follows a gradual model. The municipality must organise the operations so that on a weekday during office hours, the patient can have immediate contact with the health centre or other healthcare facility. At this point, the assessment of treatment needs is made no later than the third weekday from the initial contact. If it is considered necessary to provide treatment, it must be organised – considering the patient's state of health and predictable course of the disease – within a reasonable time. However, this must always take place no later than in three months from the assessment of treatment need. The model envisages certain exceptions which call for more urgent or less immediate access to treatment. From primary healthcare, the patient can be referred to specialised medical care, and here the assessment of treatment need must start within three weeks from the date in which the referral is received by the specialised medical care facility. Correspondingly, the treatment must be organised and started within a reasonable time, considering the urgency, but no later than six weeks from the date in which the need for treatment was diagnosed. This system also includes certain exceptions.

172. The patient must always be informed about the time in which they will receive treatment, or – if necessary – changes in the appointment and reasons thereof. The municipality or the federation of municipalities must also inform the public about the waiting times of various facilities on its Internet pages.

173. Emergency care, irrespective of the nature of treatment, must be given to all individuals, regardless of their place of residence. Urgent treatment refers to the immediate assessment and treatment required for sudden illness, injury, deterioration of a patient with a chronic disease or decrease in functional capacity, where the assessment or treatment cannot be postponed without risking a deterioration of the disease or injury. In view of emergency care, the organising authority must have on-duty-call services operating 24/7 and provided with sufficient resources and competence. Emergency care is a subjective right of the patient, meaning such care must always be accessible. Each healthcare professional is likewise bound by the obligation to provide emergency care.

174. The patient has the right to choose the unit of care within the municipality where the healthcare services are provided. It is also possible to choose services other than those organised by the municipality of residence. The possibilities of choice required by the European Union are also available to the individual. In certain circumstances, it is also possible for the individual to select the healthcare professional providing the care. If the municipality or the hospital district is not able to provide the care within the set time frame, it must organise the care by procuring it from other service providers.

175. It is also possible to seek treatment freely. The care is then provided by a licenced physician or dentist (*See* paragraphs 273–280). In this case, the patient receives a partial refund on the costs incurred, based on the sickness insurance included in the health insurance.

Chapter 2. Benefits

§1. Care Provided

176. In order to harmonise the healthcare on the national level, the Ministry of Social Affairs and Health has issued unified care guidelines. Their objective is to ensure equality in healthcare and access to treatment. All healthcare operation must be evidence-based and in line with good therapy and operative practices. When healthcare is given, a plan for the examinations, therapies and medical rehabilitation must be drafted not only on the organisation of treatment but also on the respective timetables. The plan must be made with the accord of the patient and, if necessary, with their family members or persons close to them.

177. Under the Act on the Status and Rights of Patients, the patient has the right to receive good-quality healthcare and medical care. This refers to the care required by the patient's state of health within the resources available. The right applies to the care required by the patient's state of health within the resources available. Treatment must be provided without any discrimination. Care must be organised and the patients must be treated without violating their dignity and with respect for their beliefs and privacy.

178. The patients must receive information on their state of health, the significance of the care provided, therapy options and their impacts as well as on other corresponding issues. When the information is given, due care must take to ensure that the patient understands the explanation to a sufficient degree. The information is not given against the patient's will or if such information is liable to jeopardise the patient's life or health.

179. Treatment must take place in an accord with the patient. Patients can always refuse care and therapy measures in which case they must be treated with their consent in another medically acceptable manner. If the patient is not able to decide on the therapy, their representative or next of kin must be consulted, with the objective of providing treatment that best corresponds to the patient's will. If necessary, the patient must be treated in accordance with their best interest.

180. The opinion of an underage patient must also be sought and taken into account, appropriately for their age and level of development.

181. The patient discontented with the treatment has the right to lodge a complaint addressed to the responsible director of the healthcare facility. A reply to the complaint must be given within a reasonable time. Lodging of the complaint does not influence the patient's eventual other rights.

182. The healthcare facility must have a patient ombudsman whose task is to provide advice to the patients, assist them in drafting the complaint and in making eventual claims for damages or bringing suit or initiating proceedings in relation to the exercise of the profession. Moreover, the patient ombudsman must also provide general information on patient rights and act generally for the promotion and materialisation of patient rights.

I. Promotion and Protection of Health

183. In order to promote health and well-being and prevent diseases, the municipality must organise health advice activities. The municipality is also obliged to issue birth control advice and other services to promote sexual and reproductive health. The municipalities must also implement screenings in line with the national screening programmes. The guidance and advice is primarily given in connection with other preventive services.

184. The municipal preventive healthcare includes health clinic services for pregnant women, families expecting a child as well as for babies, toddlers and children under the school age and their families. The objective is to promote the health of children as well as women during pregnancy and after childbirth through follow-ups and health promotion visits at regular intervals and according to individual needs. Health clinic services are provided at regular intervals to children of certain ages, accompanied by the parents. If necessary, the health clinic must refer the child and family to further examinations and treatment.

185. The purpose of school healthcare is to provide the pupils in basic education with health advice as well as to follow and promote health and safety and well-being in the school environment. School healthcare also includes the follow-up and promotion of the growth and development as well as health and well-being of the children at school. This is done in collaboration with the parents to support their child education work.

186. Similar to school healthcare, student healthcare is provided for students at upper secondary-level institutions as well as higher education institutions and universities located in the municipality, irrespective of the students' domicile.

187. The responsibility for organising healthcare provided for students at traditional universities and universities for applied sciences can be transferred to other system, and a specific foundation called the Finnish Student Health Service (FSHS) is, in practice, in charge of these operations as far as university students are concerned. The aim of student healthcare is to promote the health and safety of the study environment in the institute of learning as well as the well-being of the study community. It also includes the follow-up and promotion of student health and well-being as well as their study capacity. Some of the check-ups are regular health checks. Student healthcare also includes the organisation of healthcare and medical services, mental health and intoxicant abuser work, promotion of sexual health and oral healthcare. If necessary, the student must be supported and referred to further examinations and therapies.

188. The municipality is responsible for organising occupational healthcare services for the employees in the places of work situated within their territory. This obligation also applies to the self-employed persons in the municipality. Implemented in collaboration between the employers, employees and the occupational health services, the purpose of occupational healthcare is to promote the prevention of diseases and accidents, health and safety at work and in the work environment as well as the health and working and functional capacity of employees. The employer has the liability to organise occupational healthcare at its cost. In line with the above, the employer can either use municipal services or purchase them from a private service provider, or organise the occupational healthcare services autonomously.

189. The employer will collaborate with the employees or their representatives in the occupational healthcare issues. The obligation to collaborate relates particularly to the organisation and planning of the operations. Occupational healthcare must be implemented in line with the so-called good occupational healthcare practice. In cases of work or working environments with particular health risks, the employees cannot refuse, without justified reason, to subject themselves to the health check-ups organised by the occupational healthcare services. Refusal is likewise not possible if the employee's working and functional capacity must be ascertained due to certain work-related health requirements.

190. In addition to preventive occupational healthcare, the employer may also offer medical and other healthcare services to the employees.

191. For persons on old-age pension residing in the territory, the municipality must organise advisory services promoting their well-being, health and functional capacity. The purpose of these services is to promote healthy life habits and to prevent diseases and accident as well as to identify problems resulting from the declining health and functional capacity of the aged, and to support them. The municipality can also organise health-promoting check-ups and home visits with the purpose of promoting the well-being of the aged.

192. Environmental healthcare falls within the municipal responsibilities. Regulated under the Health Protection Act, the purpose of the operations is to maintain and promote the health of the municipal population and individuals as well as to prevent, reduce and eliminate the detriments in the living environments. Environmental healthcare is closely connected to administrative areas such as environmental protection, water supply services, radiation, occupational health and safety, waste management, land use and construction, physical exercise and outdoor activities and food safety. Consequently, the Health Protection Act also includes provisions on household water, waste and waste water, health requirements imposed on dwellings and other living spaces and general areas, cemeteries and burial practices.

193. The purpose of the Communicable Diseases Act is to protect people from infectious, communicable diseases. The fight against these diseases focuses on prevention, early detection and follow-up as well as on the recognition and prevention of epidemics. The Act also provides the legal framework for the examinations, treatment and medical rehabilitation of those who have fallen ill or are suspected to have a communicable disease. It also covers the operations to control of hospital infections.

194. Communicable diseases are divided into dangerous, notifiable and other infectious diseases. The municipality is responsible for organising the control of communicable diseases in its territory.

195. To prevent these diseases, the municipality must organise general voluntary vaccinations and health checks. There are specific provisions on the national vaccination programme and on the obligation to notify the adverse effects of vaccines as well as on the health checks of pregnant women. In certain cases, it is possible to organise obligatory vaccination campaigns to prevent the spreading of communicable diseases. There is also a specific register for the follow-up of the adverse effects of vaccinations.

196. Under the Communicable Diseases Act, individuals can also be treated against their will and be put in quarantine. Temporary quarantine can be imposed on a person exposed or with justified reason suspected of having been exposed to a dangerous or notifiable communicable disease. If the state of health of the person in question does not call for hospitalisation, they can be ordered to be quarantined. Goods can also be put in quarantine, and the order can be given against the will of the person involved. The quarantine must be lifted immediately when the respective conditions are no longer met.

197. If the spreading of a dangerous infectious disease cannot be prevented with the quarantine, the municipality can order that the person who has fallen or is suspected of having fallen ill to stay away from work for a maximum of six consecutive months. Correspondingly, the person can be ordered to stay away from day care or place of study. The Administrative Court may extend this period by a maximum of six months.

198. Anyone with or suspected of having a dangerous infectious disease can be isolated in medical institutions under the same conditions as they can be put in quarantine. The individual can be given the indispensable treatment to prevent the spreading of the disease, also against their will.

199. The person ordered to stay out of work, to be put in isolation or quarantine for the prevention of the spreading of a communicable disease, is entitled to receive the sickness allowance under the Health Insurance Act. Also the parent with a child under 16 years of age ordered to stay home is entitled to the allowance if the parent is prevented from working due to such quarantine. In addition to the daily allowance, the person in question is entitled to be compensated for loss of income. If goods and objects have been destroyed under the Communicable Disease Act, or they have perished or been damaged, it is also possible to receive damages for such goods and objects.

II. Medical Care

200. The production of medical care services is the municipality's responsibility although they are mostly produced by the municipal federations. Medical care services include the examinations, medical diagnosis and treatment, the medical supplies and devices needed for a chronic disease as well as the necessary medical rehabilitation. Medical care also includes the prevention and cure of diseases and alleviation of suffering. It also incorporates guidance to support the treatment adherence and self-care of patients as well as the early identification of health problems in patients requiring special support, examinations and treatment, and their referral to care and further treatment.

201. Medical care must be given in accordance with the medical needs of the patient and the uniform therapy criteria available. The treatment is given in the form of outpatient care whenever it is possible in view of patient safety. Normally, the patient must be provided with a treatment and rehabilitation plan.

202. The specialised medical care services are mostly produced by a federation of municipalities. All municipalities belong to some federation that organises specialised medical care. Some specialist-level medical care functions have been assigned to certain hospital districts with a university with a medical faculty in their area. Besides training tasks, they are also responsible for steering and advisory functions in organising the operations.

203. The federation of municipalities providing medical care must also organise the emergency services in the area. These services include the emergency care of the patients that are injured or have fallen acutely ill, and if necessary, the transportation of the patient to a more purposeful unit of care. Emergency care services maintain their preparedness and participate in the drafting of regional emergency and preparedness plans in view of disasters and special situations faced by the healthcare system. Emergency care also includes providing executive assistance to the police and certain other authorities in order for them to be able to perform their duties.

204. The patient can be provided with home nursing or hospital-at-home services. Home nursing includes the supplies required for the treatment of a chronic disease, and it is provided according to plan or temporarily in the patient's place of residence, home or corresponding place. Hospital-at-home care is an intensified form of home nursing. In this case, the medicines administered and the medical supplies used are included in the care.

III. Mental Healthcare Work

205. The purpose of mental healthcare work is to enhance the factors that protect the mental health of individuals and the community. This work also includes guidance and advisory functions as well as psycho-social support. Support can also be provided in sudden shocking situations. The term 'mental health services' refers to the examination, treatment and medical rehabilitation of mental health problems. The services must be organised primarily in the form of outpatient services. People should be supported in seeking therapy on their own initiative and in trying to cope independently. It is deemed important that the mental health services are coordinated with the social welfare services.

206. Treatment under the Mental Health Act can also be provided involuntarily. Patient rights can also be limited during involuntary care and examinations.

207. A person can be taken into involuntary psychiatric hospital care only if they are found to be mentally ill, if they are in need of therapy because of the mental disease in a way that not committing the patient to care would essentially deteriorate the mental disease or seriously endanger their or other people's health and safety as well as if any other mental health services are not suitable for use or are insufficient. All three criteria must be met.

208. Committing an under-aged person to involuntary psychiatric hospital care can take place under slightly less strict grounds. The under-aged must be treated separately from adults unless it is found to be in their best interest to act differently.

209. A person can be hospitalised for observation to examine whether there are criteria for committing the patient to treatment. The referral to such observation is based on a written medical statement. No later than the fourth day of observation from the referral, the person responsible for observing must issue a statement.

210. The decision on commitment to involuntary care is made by a senior medical officer responsible for psychiatric care. The decision must include a motivated opinion on the criteria of commitment to care. The commitment of an under-aged person to involuntary care must be immediately subjected to the approval of the Administrative Court. In all subsequent steps, the doctor acting in the previous phases of the process is prevented from giving an opinion.

211. Involuntary care must not exceed three months. If it seems imminent that therapy must be continued but the patient's consent is not obtained, a new observation statement is needed. The decision on continued therapy must be made every six months. If it becomes evident that the criteria for involuntary care are not met, the treatment must stop immediately and the patient must be discharged at their wish.

212. During criminal proceedings, the court may order a psychiatric examination on the accused. If the criteria of involuntary psychiatric care are met, the person will be committed to care. The maximum period of therapy is six months, followed by an observation statement to clarify whether the criteria for involuntary care still exist. After this, the procedure is principally the same.

213. If the court waives sentence due to the mental condition of the accused, the question about the need for psychiatric hospital care of the persons can be subjected to the Institute of Health and Welfare. If the criteria for committing the person to involuntary care exist, the person will be committed to care. If such conditions do not exist, the person must be immediately discharged, if they desire so.

214. The rights of the person taken under observation or examination or care under the Mental Health Act can be restricted. Such restrictions must be indispensable for the treatment of the disease, the safety of the patient or another person or because of a reason to limit a benefit.

215. The treatment of psychiatric or physical diseases can be imposed against the mental health patient's will only if it is indispensable to prevent a danger to their life or health. In the treatment of a mental disease, only such medically acceptable examination or treatment methods can be used against the patients will as would, if not used, seriously jeopardise the patient's or other people's health or safety. Psycho-surgical or other measures seriously and irreversible affecting the patient's integrity can only be taken upon a written consent of a person of age, unless it is a procedure that is indispensable to prevent a danger to the patient's life.

216. During treatment, if the patient opposes to care, it is possible, under certain conditions, to use indispensable and short-term means of restriction. The patient's freedom of movement can be limited and they can be prohibited from leaving the hospital or care facility. If necessary, justifiable force can be used. The patient can be isolated if, based on the behaviour or threats made, the patient would likely harm themselves or others. The patient can also be subjected to indispensable measures to hold them in place if the patient's behaviour or threats would likely lead to physical harm to other people. The patient can also be tied down with a belt. Holding, isolation and tying down are measures that must be reported to the party supervising the interests of the patient. State authorities also perform such supervision.

217. Any objects and substances that cause serious harm or danger to the patient's or other persons' health or safety or the care and order of the therapy facility can be confiscated. Money and other payment instruments can also be seized by the care facility if the patient would probably destroy them. After the treatment is over, any possessions must be returned to the patient. Certain, mostly illegal, substances can also be disposed of. The patient's belongings can be searched for substances or objects, and letters or other shipments made to the patient can be inspected without reading the message.

218. Based on justified suspicion, the patient can be subjected to a search by checking the clothing worn for dangerous substances or objects. In certain situations, the person may be subject to personal search which may be a bodily search, breathalyser or the taking a blood, urine or saliva sample.

219. The patient normally has the right to be in contact with parties outside the hospital. However, such contacts may be restricted if they are deemed to cause serious harm to the patient's therapy, rehabilitation or safety or if the restriction is indispensable for the protection of the private life of another person. In these situations, it is also possible to read an individual letter or other message sent by or addressed to the patient. The patient's communication tools and devices can be seized by the institute of care. At the end of treatment, also these objects must be returned to the owner. However, the patient must not be prevented from contacting the authorities who supervise the hospital, the international human rights bodies, legal counsel or the patient ombudsman in the hospital.

IV. Intoxicant Abuser Services

220. The aim of intoxicant abuser work is to promote the health and well-being of the inhabitants in the area. The purpose is to enhance the individual's and community's sober and healthy way of life and to reduce and eliminate the intoxicant-related factors that cause danger to health and safety. The intoxicant abuser work must be seen as a whole with a link to the social welfare and other services, including the mental health services. People can also be subjected to intoxicant abuser work on an involuntary basis (*see* paragraphs 75 and 96).

V. Rehabilitation

221. The medical rehabilitation associated with the medical care of a patient includes rehabilitation advice and guidance, assessment of the patient's functional and working capacity, rehabilitation examinations, various therapies and corresponding measures. Rehabilitation also includes services associated with various aids, adaptation training and different rehabilitation courses. Rehabilitation must constitute a functional whole with the other care provided. Rehabilitation is a comprehensive whole provided by various different actors (*see* paragraphs 109, 110, 162, 167, 200, 221, 264, 329, 336, 337, 393, 394, 399, 400, 418, 450, 491, 557–580, 587, 612, 613, 616).

VI. Medical Use of Organs, Tissues and Cells

222. The medical use of human organs, tissues and cells can relate to the treatment of a disease or injury, products manufactured for a medical use, assisted reproduction treatment or medical research as well as to the use of tissues and cells and tissue samples to purposes other than those for which they have been taken or harvested. A deceased human can be used for medical teaching and research purposes.

223. Organs, tissues and cells can be harvested from a living donor for organ transplant purposes. This always takes place with the donor's consent and it must not cause any serious health risk or harm to the donor. From the recipient patient's point of view, organ transplantation must be the most efficient available treatment. It is also required that a suitable organ or tissue or suitable cells are not available from deceased donors.

224. Organs, tissues and cells can be harvested from dead persons, and they can be stored in view of the treatment of another individual's disease or injury. However, organs, tissues or cells must not be harvested if there is justified reason to presume that the deceased would have opposed such procedure when still alive.

VII. Assisted Reproduction

225. The term 'assisted reproduction' refers to treatment whereby a human gamete or embryo is introduced to the woman's body to generate pregnancy. The legislation regulates the situations of use as well as whose gametes and embryos can be used. It is prohibited to use gametes or embryos in which the genomic content has been interfered with. This means that human genetic manipulation is prohibited. There are also other restrictions on the use of embryos. The objective in assisted reproduction is to use gametes with the donor's appearance resembling that of the respective parent of the child to be born unless the treated person otherwise wishes.

226. Normally, written consents of all parties to the assisted reproduction treatment are always required. No reward must be paid for the donation of gametes.

VIII. Abortion

227. Pregnancy can be interrupted at the request of the woman involved. Abortion may be motivated by jeopardy to the pregnant woman's life or health or by social reasons. The woman can also ask for abortion if she has become pregnant as a result of certain criminal offences. Moreover, women under 17 or over 40 years of age, or anyone with four previous childbirths, can have abortions at request. Abortion may also be motivated by a situation in which there is justified reason to assume that the child would carry a severe disease or physical defect. Moreover, either or both parents' disease, mental disorder or similar reason seriously limiting their ability to take care of a child may also qualify as the reason for abortion.

228. Abortion must be made as early as possible into the pregnancy. Normally, abortion is no longer possible after the twelfth week of pregnancy but in certain cases and with special permits, the limit is the twentieth or even the twenty-fourth week. The father of the child must also be reserved for the opportunity to be heard in the matter.

IX. Sterilisation

229. Sterilisation always requires that the person involved makes the request. A further precondition is that the woman has already given birth to three children or that the person alone or together with the spouse has three under-aged children. The person involved must be over 30 years old or in a state where a pregnancy would jeopardise her health or life. There are also other grounds that allow sterilisation.

230. Before sterilisation is performed, the person must be made aware of the significance and impacts of the procedure as well as of the other possibilities of contraception. The spouse of the person involved must be reserved the possibility to assist in the advice session. It should also be ascertained whether the sterilisation of the other spouse would be more expedient.

X. Pharmaceutical Service

231. The Medicines Act aims at maintaining and promoting a rational use of medicines. The Medicines Act refers to medicinal products, their manufacture, importation, distribution, sales and other release for consumption.

232. The Medicines Act contains definitions of a medicine, medicinal product as well as traditional herbal medicinal products, homeopathic products and reference medicinal product. The Medicines Act has links to the Narcotics Act and the Alcohol Act. Medicines may be sold to the people or otherwise released to consumption only upon authorisation, and in certain cases upon registration. The centralised marketing authorisation of medicines is granted by the EU Commission based on the opinion issued by the European Agency for the Evaluation of Medicinal Products. National authorisations are granted by the Finnish authority. Medicines can only be sold by the pharmacies, and pharmacy operations can be exercised only on the basis of a licence issued by the authorities.

§2. Amount of Benefit

233. The Finnish healthcare system is based on public services. The annual sum allocated to public healthcare is about EUR 19.8 billion (2015). The funding of the public healthcare comes from three sources: municipal tax revenue, State subsidy based on tax income and patient co-payments.

234. Parallel to this system, the health insurance system reimburses costs incurred for medicines, travelling expenses, doctors' and dentists' fees as well as examination and therapy. The annual reimbursements for medicines total about EUR 1,400 million (2016), travelling expenses 270 million, doctor's and dentist's fees 110 million and examination and therapy costs about EUR 44 million. In aggregate, the benefits account for about 13% of the healthcare expenditure. The largest role is paid by the medicines' reimbursements because the public healthcare costs only include medicines administered at outpatient clinics and in inpatient care. The health insurance system is managed and benefits are also paid by the Social Insurance Institution Kela.

235. The medicines' reimbursements are paid on medicines, clinical nutrition productions and basic creams prescribed for the treatment of a disease. The reimbursement becomes payable after the initial patient co-payment limit is reached. The initial patient co-payment is EUR 50 per the calendar year. The initial patient co-payment applies from the beginning of the year in which the individual in question becomes 19.

236. To be included in the reimbursement system, the medicine must have adopted the reimbursement status at the Pharmaceuticals Pricing Board operating under the umbrella of the Ministry of Social Affairs and Health. Kela only pays reimbursement for indispensable medication costs. If the costs for reimbursable medicines exceed the annual patient co-payment limit (EUR 610.37 in 2018), the patient will have the medicines for the rest of the year paying the EUR 2.50 patient co-payment for each medicine purchase.

237. After the initial patient co-payment, the reimbursements are divided into three categories: the basic reimbursement category rate is 40%, the lower special reimbursement category 65% and the upper special reimbursement category 100%, with EUR 4.50 patient co-payment for each purchase and product.

238. The travelling costs are normally reimbursed from the point of departure to the closest public or private healthcare physician or institute. Based on the payment commitment issued by the public system, the patient's travelling costs are reimbursed to the place of treatment. Reimbursement is also available for the travelling to a place of rehabilitation mentioned in the decision regarding the rehabilitation organised by Kela.

239. If the therapy has been provided by an operator other than the closest primary healthcare unit, the maximum reimbursement is that corresponding to the costs that would be incurred for travelling to the main healthcare station in the patient's own municipality or area covered by the local government regional authority. The travelling to a specialised medical care provider is reimbursed on the basis of the travelling costs to the closest university hospital.

240. Travelling to a private healthcare provider's place of business is reimbursed in the same way as that to public healthcare when the therapy or examination is also reimbursable.

241. Reimbursement can also be paid to a necessary accompanying person or for accommodation costs incurred for the therapy.

242. For travelling costs, Kela mainly pays the price of the cheapest means of transportation. If the patient chooses to use transportation other than the cheapest option, the healthcare unit must provide a certificate of the necessity for such means of transportation. The use of a private car is also allowed in certain cases. The patient co-payment is EUR 25 for a one-way trip. If the patient co-payments for healthcare or rehabilitation travelling exceed EUR 300 in a calendar year, the necessary travel costs in excess of the limit will be fully reimbursed.

243. Reimbursement can also be paid for some private doctors' and dentists' fees, therapies and examinations according to a determined reimbursement tariff. The costs incurred in public healthcare are not reimbursed. The basis of the reimbursements is a fixed tariff. Normally, the fees are larger than the sums in the tariff. The fees or examination and therapy prices are not regulated.

244. The reimbursement for a private doctor's or dentist's fee is according to the adopted tariff. To be eligible for reimbursement, the therapy must be necessary for the treatment of the disease.

245. Kela reimburses a part of examinations and therapies prescribed by a private doctor or dentist. The reimbursement complies with the adopted tariff. Reimbursement is also available for the costs of examinations and therapies performed or prescribed by private service providers.

246. The reimbursement is payable for therapies and examinations for which the patient has a private doctor's referral, including laboratory tests, X-rays, psychological examinations, medical procedures, radiation and chemotherapy, pathology examinations and physiotherapy. If the doctor prescribes a course of treatment, the reimbursement is payable for the maximum of fifteen sessions.

247. The tariff has been determined for each type of procedure, and there are hundreds of classified procedures.

§3. Determining Rates of Fees and Prices

248. About 7% of the operating costs of social welfare and healthcare are covered by service charges. In healthcare, the charges account for a bigger share than in social welfare, but their overall share of financing seems to be growing. The relevant legislative basis is the Act on Customer Charges in Social Welfare and Health Care.

249. When the municipality or the local government regional authority offers the services by purchasing them from a private service provider, the payments charged from the service user are the same as for the services produced by the municipality or the local government regional authority. In all other respects, the legal provision related to the payments charged for the services produced by the municipality is also applied here.

250. In the service voucher system, the payment logic is reversed. In this case, the municipal share of the payment is mostly fixed, and the service user pays the excess of the cost not covered by the service voucher issued by the municipality. In certain cases, the value of the service voucher may be proportional to the person's earnings.

251. In a broad outline, the social welfare and healthcare services can be divided into three groups based on the payments: (1) services free of charge; () services with a fixed payment; and (3) services with an earnings-related payment. In certain cases, the factual costs can be imposed which also constitute the maximum as any charges are concerned.

252. The purpose of the charges is to provide partial financing of the system but they also play a role in directing the service users towards the most appropriate services. They also impact income distribution.

253. The general idea behind the cost-free services is that it is not rational to limit but rather encourage their use. Often, the services are one-off by nature, or at least their use is limited. The preventive services play the most important role here; by encouraging people to use them, consistent future costs, for instance, in healthcare and social welfare can be avoided. For example, vaccinations against frequently occurring major public health problems are very appropriate from this perspective.

254. Services related to involuntary treatment and care are also free of charge. However, a fee is charged for some services in this group but then the motivation is that the service includes full board.

255. Services aimed at establishing factual equality are often also free of charge. For example, services offered to the disabled persons to provide them with access to societal activities and the world of work, equal to those with no disability, are free of charge.

256. The rationale of the even and fixed charges is mainly setting a low threshold for their use. In many cases, the alternative for such fixed charges could be imposing no charge at all. It is a question of purposefulness and also of funding. Typically, the fixed charge is quantified so that it discourages, to a certain extent, the unnecessary use of the service without preventing people from seeking the services.

257. Earnings-related payments are typically charged in situations where the service provides the individual with a full board or otherwise covers the indispensable living expenses, most often in institutional care. Another situation of earnings-related charges being imposed is one where the service creates conditions for earnings. For example, children's day-care payments can be motivated with this since the day care provides the parents or the single parent with an opportunity to pursue earned income.

258. A payment ceiling arrangement is in place to keep the payment burden reasonable. In 2018, the payment ceiling is EUR 683. The fees charged for services used by the under-18-year-olds are added to the payments made by the young person's guardian. When the ceiling is reached, the services are free for all the individuals who have been accumulating the sum.

259. The patient can also be exonerated from all payments or the charge can be lowered if the payment would jeopardise the individual's or their family's subsistence. This arrangement is applicable to both social welfare and healthcare.

260. The general rule covering the patient payment system is that the payments set by law are the maximum. The municipality may impose a smaller charge or choose not to impose them at all. The situation varies from municipality to municipality. The charges may be imposed on outpatient care, inpatient care, occupational healthcare and other activities. Normally, the payment is not dependent on whether the care is provided by a physician or another person.

261. In the outpatient care of the overall healthcare system, the free services generally include the preventive primary healthcare services, including the substances and certain supplies used. However, the outpatient medical care given to those over 18 years of age as well as oral healthcare, inpatient care and certain procedures may involve a charge. Emergency care is also free of charge, with the exception of patient transportation, as is psychiatric outpatient care, most of the care of respiratory paralysis patients and generally all prevention and treatment of infectious diseases. Certain other corresponding types of care are also provided free of charge.

262. For outpatient care provided at the patient's home, the charge may be imposed on the basis of a percentage rate that takes the number of family members and incomes into account. Housing services may be subject to a charge based on a compensation received under another law. For the transportation services of the severely handicapped, the municipality may impose the normal public transportation charge or a corresponding reasonable sum. The medical services provided for over-18-year-olds by the healthcare centre's outpatient care unit may be subject to a charge that may not exceed EUR 41.20 annually, or if the service user does not pay the annual charge, EUR 20.60 one-off charge. However, the EUR 20.60 payment can only be charged for the three first visits in a year at the same healthcare centre. Moreover, there are provisions regarding night-time and weekend emergency services and physiotherapy sessions. The hospital outpatient fee may not exceed EUR 41.20 per visit. There are also provisions regarding night-time and weekend activities. Day surgery is covered by exception rules.

263. For laboratory and imaging examinations performed on the basis of a private doctor's referral, with no other examinations or procedures made, the charge may be no higher than the costs incurred for producing the service. Procedure-specific payments may be imposed on oral and dental examinations and treatments while the specialised healthcare involving oral and maxillofacial procedures may, correspondingly, be subject to patient payments. The charge for patient transportation may not exceed the factual costs incurred. Courses of treatment are subject to separate provisions.

264. Patients in short-term institutional care may have to pay the maximum of EUR 22.50 per day for therapy and accommodation in a psychiatry unit, whereas the payment for other short-term institutional care may not exceed EUR 48.90 a day. However, the payments may not be imposed on those under 18 for care provided at the healthcare centre or hospital or its subunit if the therapy days in one year exceed seven. There are some exceptional rules as to certain situations involving mental health patients as well as care provided in the night and daytime. The charge for the rehabilitation provided in-house for a disabled person or rehabilitative therapy provided for the mentally disabled in the special care category may not exceed EUR 16.90 per day of therapy. The payments may not be imposed on those under 18 for care provided at the healthcare centre or hospital or its subunit if the therapy days in one year exceed seven.

265. For long-term institutional care (24-h care lasting over three months, but not in child welfare, for example) the charge is based on the individual's monthly income. The maximum charge may be 85% of the individual's income. If one of the spouses is in institutional care, the fee is 42.5% of the couple's aggregate incomes. The person must always be left with at least EUR 108 in a month (2018).

266. In occupational healthcare, the employer may be imposed a reasonable payment if occupational healthcare services are provided at the healthcare centre. The care is free of charge for the patient.

267. The disability aids given by the occupational healthcare services are normally free of charge. Likewise, the disability aids required during rehabilitation and in cases of work-related injuries are normally compensated or provided for the use of the patient. If service vouchers are used, the individual may have to pay a co-payment.

268. The payment is determined in detail but at the same time, the municipality may choose not to impose any payment. In addition, the municipality may decide to charge a reasonable fee for issues not mentioned in the law.

269. According to the provisions on service vouchers, the municipality or local government regional authority approves the service providers. The quality of the services is monitored and respective listings are maintained. The individual can choose the care service provider. The municipality issues the service voucher which can be a determined sum or income related. The value of the voucher must be reasonable and in rough proportion to the costs otherwise incurred by the municipality.

Chapter 3. Conditions

270. The regulations on the medical devices and supplies as well as on their maintained and promoted safety are contained in an act implementing certain EU directives.

271. The medical device must meet the so-called essential requirements. They must comply with the EU standards. The use of the device must not cause unnecessary danger to the health or safety of the patient, user or other person.

272. The manufacturer is responsible for the design, manufacture, packaging and markings of a medical device. The manufacturer is also liable for the risk caused by the use of the device. On the other hand, the user is liable for notifying the manufacturer of any situations of danger they have become aware of, caused or suspected of being caused by a defect or shortcoming in the device. The use and marketing of the devices are subject to supervision.

273. Healthcare professionals are divided into three categories: licenced professionals, authorised professionals and professionals with a protected occupational title. A licenced or authorised professional or a professional with a protected occupational title is entitled to practise the profession in question and to use the related occupational title.

274. The aim of the professional activities of healthcare professionals is to promote and maintain health, to prevent illness, to cure those who are ill and to alleviate their suffering. The general principle covering the exercise of the professions is that in their professional activities, healthcare professionals must employ generally accepted, empirically justified methods, in accordance with their training. The law contains an express obligation for the healthcare professionals to provide help to those in need of urgent care.

275. Licenced healthcare professionals include persons who have completed the basic medical or dental education or the specialised education and have obtained the right to practise the profession of a physician or dentist or a licenced medical specialist or dental specialist. The licence is granted to those educated in Finland as well as to the citizens of the EEA based on the medical or dentistry degree completed in the EEA States. Authorised healthcare professionals are: head dispenser pharmacist, psychologist, speech therapist, dietician, pharmacist, nurse, midwife, public health nurse, physiotherapist, laboratory technologist, radiographer, dental/oral hygienist, occupational therapist, optician or dental technician.

276. Under the Health Care Professionals Act, the licenced physician makes the decision on the medical examination, diagnosis and related treatment of the patient. Correspondingly, the dentist has the authority to decide on matters pertaining to dentistry. Licenced physicians and dentists are authorised to prescribe medicines. They are also entitled to issue medical certificates and statements.

277. Based on their training, experience and job description, other authorised healthcare professionals may have the right to initiate the treatment of the patient on the basis of the symptoms and the information available to them as well as the assessment on the need for care. In certain cases, they may also have a limited right to prescribe medicines.

278. The healthcare professionals are recorded in a national central register which is public. Moreover, the operation of the healthcare professionals is supervised and steered by State authorities.

279. These authorities can order a medical check-up or hospital examination on the healthcare professional if there is a reason to suspect that due to illness, intoxicant abuse, impaired functional capacity or corresponding reason, the said professional is unable to exercise the profession.

280. The authorities may also issue more detailed orders or guidelines to the healthcare professional as a consequence of erroneous operation, limit or cancel the licenced professional's right to exercise the profession for a definite or indefinite period of time, prohibit a professional with a protected occupational title from using such title for a definite or indefinite period of time or revoke the healthcare professionals' right to exercise the profession. The reason for such action may be the neglect of obligations, performing of tasks for which the person in question has no right or other incorrect or reprehensive action. In milder cases, the person can also be given a reprimand or their attention can be drawn to appropriate professional practice.

Part IV. Family Allowances and Benefits

Chapter 1. Field of Application

§1. Territorial Field of Application

281. The territory of the Republic of Finland as well as areas defined in the international conventions.

§2. Personal Field of Application

282. *See* 5759 and 345.

I. Maternity Package or Grant

283. The maternity package is given or the grant is paid out by virtue of the relevant Act. A woman whose pregnancy has lasted for at least 154 days and have had a health check by a physician or the health clinic prior to the fourth pregnancy month is eligible for the allowance. The maternity grant can also be given to women who adopt a child of under 18 years of age. The grant is either a maternity package or a tax-free cash benefit (EUR 170 in 2018). The value of the package is significantly higher than the sum in cash. The recipient of the grant must reside in Finland. If the family is having more than one child at a time, the grant will be higher. The maternity package and the cash benefit are always mutually exclusive. The package contains baby clothing and other useful child care items, such as a towel, bed linen, sleeping bag, mattress, changing mat and toys.

II. Child Benefit

284. Child benefit is paid for children under 17 years of age and residing in Finland. Entitlement to the child benefit starts from the birth of the child or from the date in which the child moves to Finland while no child benefit is paid if the child moves abroad.

285. The monthly sum is EUR 94.88. For the second child, the sum is EUR 104.84, for the third EUR 133.79, for the fourth EUR 153.24 and for the following children EUR 172.69 a month (in 2018).

286. A single-parent increase EUR 53.50 is added to the child benefit for each child if the parent is not married or living with a live-in partner or has separated from the spouse for the purpose of ending their life as a couple.

III. Child Maintenance Allowance

287. The parents have the obligation to maintain their underage child. If the parents live separately, the parent living with the child normally has the right to obtain child support from the other parent. The parents can either agree on the child support and its quantity or the sum can be quantified by a court of law. Child maintenance allowance is a form of support safeguarding the child's maintenance if the child cannot receive child support from the parent under the maintenance obligation. Child maintenance allowance is normally paid to the parent of the child. The full amount of the child maintenance allowance is EUR 156.39 a month.

288. The precondition for the payment of the child maintenance allowance is that there is a decision on child support. If the child is born out of wedlock and the paternity has not been officially ascertained or the child has been adopted to a single parent without a partner, the parent is eligible for child maintenance allowance. A further precondition is that the parent with the maintenance obligation has not paid the child support according to the decision or that for another reason, no child support is paid. The Social Insurance Institution Kela will require the person liable for maintenance to repay the corresponding sum afterwards.

IV. Conscript's Allowance

289. The conscript in military or in civil service and the family may receive conscript's allowance paid out by the Social Insurance Institution Kela. It can also be paid to women in voluntary military service.

290. The conscript's allowance is divided into five elements: basic allowance, housing allowance, child support, special allowance and payment of study loan interests. The full amount of the conscript's allowance is EUR 628.85 a month (in 2018).

291. The basic allowance is payable to the conscript's spouse or child. The sum corresponds to the national pension. The housing allowance is paid to the conscript or to a family member entitled to receive it if they are, for example, paying rent during the service. The housing allowance covers the factual housing expenses.

292. The child support under the conscript's allowance is paid to the child entitled to receive child support and it corresponds to the factual child support sum that the conscript should pay to the under-aged child but is not able to do so during the service. The special allowance under the conscript's allowance is a discretionary element payable to a family member of the conscript. The conscript's allowance can also cover the interest of the conscript's study loan if they fall due for payment during the service or during the month in which the service ends.

V. Child Maintenance Credit

293. According to the Income Tax Act, the income tax payable by the taxpayer to the State is subject to a child maintenance credit which amounts to one-eighth of the amount paid by the said taxpayer as child support during the tax year; however, maximum sum is EUR 80 per underage child.

VI. Daily Childcare

294. The primary form of children's day care is the one provided under the Early Childhood Education Act. It is arranged at day-care centres, in the form of family day care, playground activities or other forms of caretaking. The right to day care applies to children under the compulsory education age and, under special circumstances and as required by older children, if the care has not been arranged otherwise.

295. Early childhood education takes place in day-care centres in specific facilities (kindergartens, day-care centres, nurseries). Based on the need for special care and education, day care can also be organised in special day-care centres. Family day care is organised in a private home or other home-like care facility. Playground activities and other day care can be organised in a particular place. The precondition is that the parents are not receiving any parental allowance.

296. Early childhood education should be organised so that it provides a suitable place for the child's care and education and continuous care during the time of the day in which it is needed. The purpose of day care is to support the child's parents in their educational task and, together with the homes, promote the balanced development of the child's personality. The general objective of day care is to promote the child's physical, mental and social development, complemented by aspects related to the environment and the child's personality.

297. Children have the subjective right to receive twenty hours of early childhood in a week. If both parents are involved in full-time work, study or self-employed or other own work, the child has the subjective right to full-time early childhood education. The right to early childhood education can be extended if the work or search for work of the parents so requires. However, the child must receive full-day early childhood education if it is necessary in view of the child's development, need for support or family circumstances or if it is otherwise in the best interest of the child.

298. Early childhood education is closely linked to the pre-primary education which constitutes part of basic education. In organising the pre-primary education, children's possibilities to have early childhood education must also be taken into account. A child in pre-primary education must also have part-time early childhood education.

299. The municipality is obliged to organise early childhood education. It must either be arranged or supervised by the municipality, and it must be offered to the extent and in the forms that are required based on the needs of the municipality. Early childhood education must be provided in Finnish, Swedish or in the Sami language. The municipality can arrange for the services or procure them from a private service provider. The Valvira and the Regional State Administrative Agencies monitor the quality of early childhood education and may prohibit the provision of day-care services if the place maintained by the service provider or the care provided is found to be inappropriate or inadequate. Collaborating with the parents, every child must be drafted an early education plan, also hearing the child.

300. Day care is provided against a fee but the municipality may decide to charge a smaller fee than the maximum, or not to charge any fee. When determining the fee, the family's taxable earnings and capital income as well as tax-free income are taken into account. If necessary, average income or estimated income is used for the calculation. Income of expense compensation type is not taken into consideration. The monthly fee is determined so that the income in excess of an income limit, depending on the family size, is taken into account according to a determined percentage. The maximum fee is EUR 289 a month (2018). If several children are in day care, the fee regards the youngest child and the fee for the following child is 50% of the fee payable for the first child, however, not more than EUR 145. The fee for the following children is 20% of the sum paid for the youngest child. The fee for the children in partial day care is normally proportionate to the duration of the daily care. Sums lower than EUR 27 are not charged.

VII. Support to Childcare

301. Under the Employment Contracts Act, the employee is entitled to take childcare leave to mind their own child or another child permanently living in their household until the child's third birthday.

302. Childcare leave can be taken in a maximum two periods of at least one month. The employer and the employee can also agree on the leave differently. Childcare leave can be taken by only one parent or carer at a time. During maternity or parental leave, the other parent or carer can take one period of childcare leave.

303. A child not yet in the compulsory education age but no longer covered by the parental allowance has the right to receive municipal early childhood education. The alternative to this is an arrangement whereby the parents receive child home care allowance or private day-care allowance. These forms of support are funded by the municipality. Certain municipalities complement the statutory home care allowance by a municipality-specific supplement to the allowance. The child home care allowance is paid to families where a child under three years of age is not in a day care organised by the municipality. In this case, the parents are responsible for organising the childcare. The elements of child home care allowance are basic home care allowance and the home care supplement. The basic home care allowance is a standard sum while the home care supplement depends on the family's income. Parents receiving the home care allowance are not obliged to take care of the child at home but they can organise the care at their own discretion.

304. The child home care allowance is also paid for the siblings of the child under three if they are not yet in compulsory education or in municipal day care.

305. Employees are entitled to have partial childcare leave to take care of their own child or another child living permanently in their household. The right remains in force until the second school term of the child in basic education, and in certain situations beyond this point of time. The precondition is that the employee has been employed by the same employer for a total of six months in total during the previous twelve months. The employee may be entitled to receive partial home care allowance (*see* paragraph 322).

306. The parent of a disabled or chronically ill child in need of special care or caretaking may be entitled to partial home care allowance until the child is 18 years old. The two parents cannot be on childcare leave simultaneously.

307. The employer and the employee have relatively free hands to agree on the partial childcare leave arrangements. However, the employer may refuse to agree on the leave or consent to it on particular grounds only.

308. The employee will always have the right to take one partial childcare leave period in a calendar year. The length and time of the leave are determined on the basis of the proposal made by the employee. In this case, the childcare leave takes place by shortening the daily working hours to six hours. The employee may interrupt the partial childcare leave through an agreement with the employer.

309. To obtain the flexible home care allowance, the parent must work no more than thirty hours on average per week, or maximum 80% of the full working hours. To obtain the allowance, one criterion must be filled. The parent must have a contract of employment of tenure, a self-employed person or a recipient or a grant with a valid pension insurance.

310. The flexible home care allowance can be applied for immediately after the parental allowance period. It can be received until the child is three. The parent makes an agreement with the employer on the working hours. Both the child's father and mother can receive the flexible home care allowance. However, they need to be absent from work and take care of the child at separate times. The flexible home care allowance can be obtained simultaneously with the private care allowance or if the child is in municipal care.

311. Families with children under the school age are eligible to receive this allowance if they hire a caretaker or other private day-care provider to take care of the child. The private day-care allowance is constituted by the basic home care allowance and the home care supplement, with the latter adjusted to the family's incomes.

312. The precondition for private day-care allowance is that the child is not in municipal day care. However, the child has the right to participate in pre-primary education. The caretaker must be approved by the municipality.

313. The private day-care allowance is paid directly to the caretaker and the family pays the eventual difference between the care charge and the day-care allowance. However, the allowance may not exceed the care charge. If the caretaker is a private person, the child's parent is the caretaker's employer, and an employment contract must be signed with the caretaker.

314. When the employee's child or another child living permanently in the household falls acutely ill, the employee has the right to take temporary childcare leave to arrange for the care or take care of the child. The leave must not exceed four working days at a time. The child must be under 10 years old.

315. The employee has the right to be temporarily absent from work if their immediate presence is imperative due to an unpredictable and compelling reason resulting from a sickness or accident in the family.

Chapter 2. Dependent Children

316. According to Finnish law, a person under 18 is a child. Under the Act on Child Maintenance, the child has the right to be maintained by the parents or other guardians. However, children older than this have the right to maintenance if they study. The practical importance of this provision has little legal weight. The after-care of child welfare must be available to a child even after the 18-year milestone.

317. A child of 15 is able to control his or her earnings. A child of that age also has an independent right of speech in the decision-making of administrative law nature. 15-year-olds are also liable for their action in terms of the penal law. In teaching and education, the 15-year-olds have the right to apply for a correction of a decision related to student assessment.

318. The status and rights of children follow the UN Convention on the Rights of the Child. A child of age 12 must be heard, and the opinion of children younger than that must be found out. A child over age 12 can be taken into custody only upon the decision of a court of law if the child contests the taking into custody. At this age, children can independently appeal a child welfare decision regarding them in person. The age of 12 is the threshold for a change in the child's status in certain other child welfare issues. Moreover, if the child is against the visiting rights of a parent without custody, the visit cannot be enforced.

319. The provisions on the position of children are contained not only in general legislation but also in the Constitution (equal treatment of children and their possibility to impact issues that concern them, the protection of children against visual programmes as well as the support to those in charge of their care to safeguard their well-being and growth).

Chapter 3. Amount of the Benefit

320. The child home care allowance is EUR 338.34 a month. The allowance for other siblings under three years is EUR 101.29 a month and EUR 65.09 for those over three years. The full home care supplement will be paid if the family's monthly income is not in excess of the limit determined on the basis of family size. If the income limit is reached, the deduction is made to the full home care supplement using a proportionate percentage rate.

321. The child home care support is normally adjusted taking the other supports into consideration. Parental allowance days will reduce the home care supplement element of the child home care allowance. Employment security constitutes income and may have an impact on the home care supplement. Study allowances will not influence the home care allowance but the latter will be taken as income in the calculations for the study allowance income thresholds.

322. The sum paid during the partial home care leave is EUR 96.89 month. This sum is payable for one child only.

323. The flexible home care allowance is paid to a parent working thirty hours a week or less, taking care of the child under three years for the rest of the week. The amount of the allowance is based on the factual working hours. The sum will be EUR 241.19 a month when the working hours do not exceed 22.5 hours a week or maximum 60% of the normal full-time working hours and EUR 160.80 a month when the workings hours are between 22.5 and 30 hours a week or 60%–80% of the normal full-time working hours. The flexible home care allowance is paid for one child at a time.

324. The private childcare support includes an allowance of EUR 172.25 per month per child. The lower rate of home care allowance payable to a child in pre-primary education is EUR 63.38 a month. The amount of the home care supplement is maximum EUR 144.85 a month per child, and the family can also receive a municipality-specific supplement depending on their municipality of residence.

325. The unemployment and pension benefits include an increase for children. A disabled child is eligible for disability benefits.

Chapter 4. Payment

326. Normally, all family supports are paid on a monthly basis to a banking account. They are paid by the Social Insurance Institution Kela.

Part V. Incapacity to Work

Chapter 1. Field of Application

§1. Territorial Field of Application

327. See 57–59.

§2. Personal Field of Application

328. See 57–59.

Chapter 2. Benefits

329. In Finland, sickness, maternity, paternity, parenthood, child disease or disability, rehabilitation and long-term disability are reasons for disability entitling the person concerned to receive benefits. In certain cases, those surviving a deceased person may be entitled to receive benefits.

§1. Funeral Benefit

330. The funeral benefit is only included in the seamen's pension scheme.

§2. Incapacity to Work

I. Wage Earners

331. Both the public and private sector wage and salary earners receive benefits due to the situations mentioned in 57–59.

II. Self-employed

332. All self-employed persons receive benefits due to the situations mentioned in 57–59.

III. Other Persons

333. In principle, all persons permanently residing in the country receive benefits due to the situations mentioned in 57–59.

Chapter 3. Certification of Incapacity to Work

334. The sickness allowance can be paid to a person between 16 and 67 years of age, and unable to perform the normal work due to the sickness. When the employee's sickness is prolonged, the employer, the employee and the occupational healthcare service collaborate to establish the employee's potential continuation in the former work. The occupational healthcare physician must estimate the remaining working capacity of the employee no later than after ninty weekdays of sickness allowance. The statement by the occupational healthcare physician is a prerequisite for the continued payment of the sickness allowance after ninty days.

335. The purpose of the partial sickness allowance is to support the person in question to maintain their job or to return to it. It is intended for employees or self-employed persons between 16 and 67 years of age in full-time work. The criteria for receiving the partial sickness allowance are mainly the same as those applicable to the normal sickness allowance. The general criterion for the partial sickness allowance is that the person concerned is unable to work. However, they must be able to perform a part of the work-related duties without jeopardising their health and recovery. The working hours must be reduced by at least forty and no more than 60%, and the respective agreement between the employer and the employee must be in force throughout the partial sickness allowance period. The same working hour reduction requirement applies to self-employed persons.

336. Parents who need to stay away from work to care for their sick or disabled child under 16 years are eligible for the special care allowance. The criterion is that the parent participates in the care or rehabilitation of the child under 7 years, either in a hospital, outpatient clinic or rehabilitation or adjustment training course. Contributing to the care of a severely sick child between 7 and 15 years in a hospital, outpatient clinic or rehabilitation also entitles the parent to receive the special care allowance. Care at home can be provided to a severely sick child of under 16 years.

337. When it is a question of a compensation for loss of income resulting from the fact that the parent is prevented from taking care of the child, the special care allowance can be received for the care and rehabilitation of the own child, adoptive child, spouse's or live-in partner's child or a child that the person has factually cared for as a parent would. The degree of severity of the child's care is determined on the basis of a statement by the attending physician.

338. The general purpose of the family leaves under the Employment Contracts Act could be defined as the reconciliation of work and family life. The particular purpose is to guarantee the possibilities for the parents, mostly parents of small children, to take care of their child.

339. The employee is entitled to have leave from work during the maternity (105 weekdays), special maternity, paternity (54 weekdays) and parental leave (158 weekdays) periods referred to in the Health Insurance Act. The length of the leaves is determined according to the Act, and the employer must grant the leave. As regards the parental leave, there are special provisions according to which the employee has the right to take it in maximum two parts which must be at least twelve weekdays long. Paternity leave can partly coincide with other leave. The duration of the special maternity leave depends on the circumstances. For the benefits payable during the leaves, *see* 351–362.

340. Working during the maternity and parental allowance payment periods is regulated by particular provisions. With the consent of the employer, the employee can work during the maternity allowance period if this will not jeopardise her, the foetus's or the newly born child's health. However, two weeks prior to and after the anticipated childbirth are covered by an absolute ban of work. Both the employer and the employee have the right to interrupt the work performed during the maternity allowance period.

341. The employer and the employee can also agree on the conditions of part-time work performed during the parental leave. In this case, the employee is entitled to receive partial parental allowance in line with the Health Insurance Act (*see* paragraph 357). For a justified reason, the employee has the right to interrupt such part-time work and to either return to parental leave or to follow their earlier working hours if no agreement is found on the interruption of the part-time work or on the change of the terms.

342. The employer must be informed about the maternity, paternity and parental leave no later than two months prior to the beginning of the leave. However, the communication for a leave not exceeding twelve weekdays can be given one month prior to the leave. For a justified reason, the employee can change the time and length of the leave by notifying the employer accordingly.

343. The employer is not liable to pay the employee for the absences under the Employment Contracts Act. As an exception to the liability for the expenses, the employer must reimburse the loss of earnings incurred by a pregnant employee for medical examinations prior to the childbirth if such examinations cannot be made outside the working hours.

344. When the family leave ends, the primary right of the employee is to return the old job. If this is not possible, the employer must offer work corresponding to the old work and complying with the employment contract, and if neither of these paths is possible, other work that corresponds to the employment contract.

345. The special conditions for obtaining the parenthood allowances are related to residence in Finland. In order to receive the allowance, the person in question must have resided in Finland for 180 days immediately preceding the childbirth, or in cases of adoption, before the child is placed in the insured person's home. The time of being insured in another European Union Member State and residence in a State applying the EU legislation is equivalent to the time of residence in Finland. The provisions on the allowances related to parenthood are also applied to the insured who, without concluding marriage, lives permanently with the child's mother in a shared household in marriage-like circumstances. However, this does not apply to an insured that, without concluding marriage, lives permanently with the adoptive parent in a shared household in marriage-like circumstances. The parties of a registered partnership may receive parenthood allowances with certain exceptions.

346. Long-term incapacity to work, see disability pensions 557–580 and 586–588.

Chapter 4. Benefits

§1. Wage Earners

347. The maximum length of the sickness allowance period is 300 days for the same disease or condition. The payment of the sickness allowance starts only after the waiting period which is normally the day in which the person falls ill and the nine following weekdays. If the same disease recurs, the payment of the allowance starts from the following weekday. The allowance is paid for six weekdays in a week. According to the Finnish Constitution, the person must receive the basic social allowance during sickness. The maximum duration of the sickness allowance being 300 weekdays, a situation may arise where the person is not entitled to the sickness allowance or the disability pension, or has not yet been granted a pension. In order to secure basic subsistence under these circumstances, the person may receive a benefit under the Unemployment Allowances Act if he or she meets the respective criteria. In this case, the unemployment security is used to patch up the basic rights problem caused by the maximum duration of the payments under the Health Insurance.

348. Normally, the allowance cannot be combined with another simultaneous form of social benefit.

349. The sickness allowance amount is based on the confirmed taxable earned income. It is either a proportional share of the person's pay or the minimum allowance.

350. The sickness allowance is based on the earnings confirmed in the tax assessment for the preceding year. In the calculation of the allowance, the expenses incurred in acquiring the income will be deducted, including travelling expenses or union and unemployment fund membership fees. The earnings will be adjusted to correspond to the level of the year in which the allowance is granted. It is also possible to account for an increase in the person's income by at least 20%. In this case, the calculation is based on the aggregate earnings for the six months preceding the sickness. In certain cases the decision is based on an estimate.

351. The sickness allowance amounts to 70% of the 1/300 part of the insured person's annual earnings if they do not exceed EUR 30,394 in a year. However, the minimum earnings are EUR 1,427. For the earnings in excess of EUR 30,394, the allowance is 20% of the 1/300 part of the annual earnings. The minimum allowance is EUR 24.64. The sums refer to the year 2018.

352. Partial sickness allowance can be paid for a period of 120 days. The partial sickness allowance is 50% of the full allowance.

353. The maximum duration of the special care allowance is sixty weekdays per child. The period can be extended by thirty weekdays. For weighty medical reasons, the payment period can be extended even further.

354. The parental allowances include maternity allowance, special maternity allowance, paternity allowance, parental allowance and partial parental allowance. The general criteria for determining the allowances related to parenthood are the same applied to sickness allowance. However, the recipients of the allowances related to parenthood need not meet the working criterion. The employer's right to receive the allowances related to parenthood is the same as those applied to sickness allowance.

355. All parental allowances are calculated in the same way. If the annual income is lower than EUR 10,562, the allowance is EUR 24.64 for each weekday (also to those without any income). In case of those with the annual income between the above and EUR 37,168, the allowance is 70% of 1/300 of the annual income. Finally, the percentage is 40% if the annual income up to EUR 57,183 and 25% in excess of that.

356. For the first fifty-six days, the maternity allowance is higher. The minimum allowance of EUR 24.64 is paid to those with the annual income up to EUR 8,215. Beyond that up to the annual income of EUR 57,183, the calculation criteria is 90% of 1/300 of the annual income. If the income is higher, the applied percentage is 32.5%.

357. The partial parental allowance is 50% of the normal allowance. It is calculated separately for each parent.

358. The allowances paid to adoptive parents correspond to the benefits received by biological parents. The adoption support is EUR 1,00–EUR 4,500 depending on the country of origin of the adoptive child.

§2. Self-employed Workers

359. In case of entrepreneurs and self-employed persons, the earnings constituting the basis for their sickness allowance, special care allowance and parental allowance are determined on the basis of the reported income confirmed for the purposes of the self-employed persons' pension or farmers' pension insurance application. For the rest, the duration and calculation of these benefits correspond to that of wage earners, *see* 347–358).

360. The recipients of grants for artistic or scientific work will be paid the sickness allowance on the basis of the income they have reported to the system.

§3. Other Persons

361. The minimum allowance payable to someone without work after fifty-five days, or if the earnings-adjusted allowance would result under the minimum, is EUR 24.64 for six days a week (in 2018).

362. The unemployed, those on rehabilitation support and students will receive the maternity allowance following particular transitional provisions. They are tied to their earlier social benefits.

Chapter 5. Conditions

363. The general criterion of eligibility for the sickness allowance is that the insured has had at least EUR 1,427 of annual earned income (at the 2018 level). Moreover, the insured must meet the work criterion. To be eligible for the sickness allowance, the person concerned must not have been, on his or her own account, out of work or employment uninterruptedly for three consecutive months prior to the disability for work. However, if the working criterion is not met, the person will still have the right to receive the minimum sickness allowance if the disability for work has persisted for at least fifty-five consecutive days. The work criterion is met not only by employees, entrepreneurs or self-employed persons but also by full-time students, unemployed jobseekers and homemakers as well as during certain statutory leaves. To receive the allowance, the person in question must be between 16 and 67 years of age, and unable to perform their own or corresponding work.

364. Sickness allowance is paid to the employer to the extent that the insured is entitled to receive pay or corresponding remuneration based on the employment. Sickness allowance may also be received in certain special situations. Those ordered to stay away from work, in isolation or under quarantine in order to prevent the spreading of a communicable disease as provided by the Communicable Diseases Act may be entitled to the sickness allowance. In these cases, the same criteria may be applied to the parent or other person caring for a child under 16 years of age. Sickness allowance may also be paid on the basis of the Act on Medical Use of Human Organs and Tissues. This would apply, for example, to someone being unable to work as a result of donating a kidney or other organ.

365. The precondition for the maternity allowance is that the woman's pregnancy has lasted at least 154 weekdays. The allowance is paid for 105 weekdays. The right to receive maternity allowance starts no earlier than fifty weekdays and no later than thirty weekdays prior to the expected date of delivery. If the pregnancy has terminated earlier than 30 weekdays prior to the expected date of delivery, the maternity allowance is still paid for 105 weekdays. If the payment of the allowances starts earlier than thirty days prior to the expected date of delivery, it is required that the insured is not in employment or performing other work of her own except for the household work at home.

366. The special maternity allowance can be paid to a pregnant insured whose work-related tasks or conditions include exposure to a chemical substance, radiation or infectious disease or similar factor that jeopardises her or the embryo's health. A further condition for the special maternity allowance is that no other work can be arranged for the insured and that for this reason, she must be absent from work. The special maternity allowance period starts when the woman is prevented from working due to the danger factor and ends when the right to regular maternity allowance starts.

367. During the maternity allowance period, the woman can work and receive the allowance. For the days of work, the minimum allowance is paid. Working on

Sundays does not impact the maternity allowance because it is paid for weekdays only. Receiving pay during the maternity leave causes the maternity allowance to be paid to the employer.

368. Paternity allowance can be received during the paternity leave for the maximum of fifty-four weekdays. The paternity allowance can be obtained for 1–18 weekdays during the maternity and parental allowance periods. The criterion for receiving the paternity allowance is that the father cares for the child at home. During this time, the father must not work or study full-time. The allowance can be paid until the child is 2 years old, or two years have passed since adoption.

369. The father must live together with the mother of the child in a shared household. If the parents live at different addresses, the paternity allowance can be paid if the situation is due to work. However, if the father lives at a separate address due to the breach of the relationship, the paternity allowance is not paid. The father may be eligible for paternity allowance even if the mother has not the right to receive the parental allowance. Paternity allowance can also be paid to the party in a registered partnership adopting the spouse's child. This paternity allowance is not dependent on the gender, and it is called 'benefit corresponding to paternity allowance'.

370. Parental allowance can be paid either to the child's father or mother. The allowance period starts after the maternity leave and it lasts for 158 weekdays. The criterion for obtaining the parental allowance is that the mother has had a health check after the birth of the child. The child's parents can divide the parental allowance period so that each of them can have no more than two allowance periods of at least eighteen weekdays. The father's right to parental allowance is not dependent on the mother's right. The provisions of parental allowance are applied to the child's father and adoptive father who is married to and living with the child's mother and is not living separately from her due to a breach in the relationship. The parents' cohabitation and marriage are treated equally. Both parents cannot be on parental leave at the same time, except for situations of several children born at the same time.

371. The parental allowance period is extended by sixty weekdays per child starting from the second child if several children are born at the same time.

372. Partial parental allowance can be paid when the parents divide the responsibility for childcare and simultaneously work part-time. They need to have made at least two-month agreements on part-time work with their employers.

373. Adoptive parents' benefits correspond to those obtained by birth parents, with the exception of maternity allowance, which cannot be paid. However, the parental allowance period applicable to adoptive parents is longer. The benefit will always be paid for at least 200 weekdays or until 234 weekdays have passed since the child's birth. The parental allowance is payable when the child adopted is under 7 years. Parental allowance can also be partial parental allowance.

374. The adoptive father can receive the paternity allowance and take the paternity leave on the same conditions applied to any father. The adoption can also take place within the family if one parent adopts the spouse's child or adoptive child. In a registered partnership, the child adopted must not be older than 1 year for the adoptive parent to receive the adoptive parent's parental allowance. A spouse in a registered partnership can also receive paternity allowance and if the beneficiary is a woman, the term used is 'benefit corresponding to the paternity allowance'.

375. Adoptive parents can also receive adoption support for foreign adoption proceedings.

Chapter 6. Accumulation Rules

376. Different benefits cannot be accumulated, except for the paternal allowance which can coincide with the maternity or parental allowance for a determined period of time.

Part VI. Industrial Accidents and Occupational Diseases

377. The rationale of the legislation on industrial accidents and occupational diseases is to compensate the losses directly associated with an accident or an occupational disease contracted at work. In principle, the accident insurance provides full coverage for the losses incurred. The insurance provides compensation for loss of income in case of short-term and long-term disability or death as well as the reimbursement for expenses incurred for a disease. Compensation is also paid for permanent handicap.

Chapter 1. Field of Application

§1. Territorial Field of Application

378. The workers' compensation insurance covers accidents and occupational diseases in the work performed in Finland, with certain exceptions. The Act is not applied to work performed by an employee in Finland if the employee is not subject to the EU social security regulations or the Finnish legislation on the basis of a social security convention binding to Finland. The Act is not applied to the work performed in Finland by an employee from a third country if the work in question is road transport traffic work, performed by the employee mostly outside Finland, the employee does not reside in Finland, the employer is not domiciled in Finland and the Finnish legislation is not applied according to the EU social security regulations. Moreover, the Act is not applied to an employee who is in Finland for a meeting or artistic performance or similar short-term visit, with the purpose of the visit related to the employee's work abroad. It is also required that the employee does not reside in Finland, the employer is not domiciled in Finland and the Finnish legislation is not applied according to the EU social security regulations.

379. The Act is applied to the work performed by the employer outside Finland if that employee is subject to the Finnish legislation on the basis of the EU social security regulations or the Finnish legislation on the basis of a social security convention binding to Finland. The Act will also be applied to work performed by the employee as an expat employee in a third country, provided that the employee is working either for the Finnish employer sending him or her abroad or for a foreign company which is part of the same financial entity (group of companies), the employee's employment relationship with the Finnish company continues after the foreign assignment and the employee is covered by the Finnish social security legislation when leaving Finland for the assignment. However, the Act does not apply to the employee whose insurance company has, upon the application made by the employer, decided that the employee is no longer covered by the insurance. The prerequisite for the decision is that the work abroad is no longer of temporary nature and it has lasted over two years. The decision is applied starting from the beginning of the calendar year following which it becomes legally valid.

§2. Personal Field of Application

380. The legislation on accidents and occupational diseases or the Workers' Compensation Insurance Act will be applied to a person in employment or in seaman employment or in a tenured position with the State, a municipality or other public sector position of public law nature.

381. A person working against consideration in a limited liability company or other corporation in a leading position is comparable to an employee although not in an employment relationship with the limited liability company or other corporation if not in a relationship with the company, as specified in detail in the law, that would qualify him or her as an entrepreneur. A leading position refers to the position of a managing director, board member or other similar position or other corresponding and factual controlling position in a limited liability company or other corporation.

382. Family members (spouse as well as persons in an ascending or descending family line living in the same household) are covered by the Act in certain circumstances.

383. Persons with the pension insurance as per the Self-employed Persons' Pension Insurance Act are entitled to have an insurance against accidents taking place in their self-employment. The insurance will cover the work also covered by the respective Pension Insurance Act. The insurance cannot enter into force retroactively.

384. The Workers' Compensation Insurance Act is not applied to the farmer work or work performed by a recipient of a grant, covered by the Act on Farmers' Occupational Accident Insurance. The Act is not applicable to sports activities. Both groups are covered by separate legislation. In the case of farmers, it is difficult to distinguish the working hours and place of work from their homes, so the definition of an accident is broader in their case. Students are subject to a separate act as regards the compensation for injuries or diseases originating in circumstances that resemble work. There is also separate legislation on military accidents, covering not only conscripts but also those liable to work or taken to work. Military accident compensations are similar to those paid on the basis of the Workers' Compensation Insurance Act.

385. There are also labour market-based group life insurance policies where a one-off compensation is payable after the death of an employee.

386. The healthcare system includes a particular patient injury arrangement whereby the patient's personal injury is compensated if it is probable that it is caused by examinations, therapies or similar treatments or a neglect associated with them, on the condition that experienced healthcare professionals would have examined, treated or otherwise handled the patient differently, thereby probably avoiding the injury. Compensation is also payable for injuries caused by faulty devices. Another healthcare-related arrangement, the pharmaceuticals injury insurance, compensates for personal injuries caused by the use of pharmaceuticals for pharmacotherapy purposes.

Chapter 2. Concept of 'Industrial Accident'

§1. Accident

387. The definition of an 'industrial accident' comprises the concept of accident and the circumstances whereby the accident can be regarded to be work related. An industrial accident is one that has caused an injury or disease to an employee at work, work-related circumstances at the place of work or in the area belonging to the workplace, in commuting from home to work or vice versa, or running the employer's errands or when trying to safeguard or safe the employer's property or, in the context of the work, human life.

388. An injury is a sudden and unexpected event caused by an external factor that causes the employee to suffer an injury or disease.

§2. Link to the Contract of Employment

389. To meet the criteria of an industrial accident, the event must have a connection to the employment. Therefore, the accident must be one taking place at work or in circumstances resulting from work at the workplace or in an area that is part of the workplace, during commuting to and from home to the workplace or when the employee is performing something for the employer. A sufficient connection is also constituted by the fact that the accident takes place while the employee tries to protect or save the employer's property or human lives in connection with work. The connection between the accident and work is not covered by particular criteria related to time or place. Work may be done during regular working hours, during overtime or an assignment. Correspondingly, the scope of coverage of the insurance is relatively wide as relates to the circumstances attributable to work. However, the connection to work must be there.

§3. Accidents on the Way to Work.

390. *See* 387.

Chapter 3. Concept of 'Occupational Disease'

391. The term 'occupational disease' refers to a condition that has probably been mainly caused by the employee being exposed to a physical, chemical or biological factor at work, in the area of the place of work or during training covered by the scope of application of the law. If the Act is applied to the employee performing the work in his or her own apartment or in a place other than the workplace organised by the employer, the exposure must be caused by the work-related tasks of the employee.

Chapter 4. Medical Care

392. The person injured in a work-related accident will have a reimbursement of the patient payment for the care provided in public medical care. If the injured person has the right to receive indemnity for medical care, the insurance company must pay the full medical care costs incurred by the municipality or the local government regional authority that has organised the care. Correspondingly, the insurance company will reimburse the care costs incurred for necessary private medical care.

393. The reimbursable medical care includes emergency care, examination, diagnosis and treatment of the injury or disease, medicines and medical supplies as well as medical rehabilitation given as a form of therapy, as well as disability aids.

394. The injured with impaired working or functional capacity or earning potential due to the accident will receive indemnity for rehabilitation costs. Rehabilitation costs will also be indemnified if it is likely that the working or functional capacity or earning potential of the injured may later be impaired to an essential degree.

Chapter 5. Incapacity to Work

395. The injured has the right to receive a per diem allowance for one year starting from the date of the accident if the person in question is unable to work, either fully or partly, due to the accident. However, if the decrease in working capacity is less than 10%, the injured will not be entitled to receive the allowance. Moreover, the allowance can be granted if the work-related earnings have diminished by at least 1/20 of the minimum annual work-related earnings. The per diem allowance will be paid for each calendar day, excluding the date of the injury. However, the allowance is not paid if the injured has not been fully or partly incapable of working for at least three subsequent days, excluding the date of the injury.

396. If the occupational disease manifests itself when the injured is on an old-age or invalidity pension and the exposure has taken place before retirement, the right to receive the allowance is assessed on the basis of the last work the person in question was involved in before retirement. If the injured is partly incapable of performing the work, the allowance paid will be less than the full sum and proportionate to the rate of impairment of the working capacity.

397. The allowance is based on the annual work-related earnings once twenty-eight days have passed from the injury, excluding the date of the accident. The allowance based on the annual work-related earnings is 1/360 of the injured person's annual earnings.

398. The injured has the right to receive the industrial injuries pension starting from one year from the accident if the ensuing decrease in the working capacity is estimated to be at least 10%. Moreover, the allowance can be granted if the work-related earnings have diminished by at least 1/20 of the minimum annual work-related earnings. In the assessment of impairment of the person's working capacity, another factor taken into consideration is the individual's remaining capacity earn income through work that he or she can reasonably be expected to cope with. In this case, the injured person's training, earlier activities, age, place of residence and other similar factors are taken into consideration. To determine the impairment of the capacity to work, the causal relationship between the decrease in earnings and the occurrence of damage must be established. If the working capacity of the injured is partly impaired, the industrial injuries pension payable is the proportionate part of the full pension corresponding to the rate of impairment.

399. The industrial injuries pension (disability pension) can be granted either for a determined period or for the time being. The pension cannot be granted for an indefinite time until the need for and possibilities of rehabilitation have been clarified. The maximum annual amount of the disability pension is 85% of the annual work-related earnings until the injured person is 65 years old, and after that, it will be 70% of the annual work-related earnings. The amount of the pension already paid will be increased from the beginning of the calendar year in which five full calendar years have passed calculating from the beginning of the calendar year following the accident. The percentage of the increase is determined on the basis of the age of the injured at the beginning of the calendar year the pay is increased.

400. The injured is entitled to receive a rehabilitation allowance during vocational rehabilitation. However, the per diem or the disability pension will not be paid for the same period of time. For one year from the accident date, the rehabilitation allowance is the same as the full daily allowance, irrespective of the impairment of the working capacity. After that, the rehabilitation allowance corresponds to the full disability pension, irrespective of the impairment of the working capacity. The allowance will be smaller if the injured person works.

401. If a full-time student is injured, the per diem or the invalidity pension corresponds to the payments for full incapacity to work if mainly the capacity to study is prevented. However, the per diem or the pension will correspond to half of the compensation for the loss of income payable for full incapacity to work, if the injury limits the capacity to study to a significant degree.

402. The annual work-related earnings constituting the basis for the compensation are the injured person's earnings at the annual level as per the moment of the injury. The earnings are calculated on the basis of the work-related earnings obtained by the injured from his or her employments at the moment of the injury during the year preceding the injury. The annual work-related earnings can be adjusted if they had been exceptionally small.

Chapter 6. Death

403. If the injured dies as a result of the accident, the survivor's pension and the funeral grant will be paid to the family beneficiaries. The survivor's pension consists of the spouse's pensions and the orphan's pension. The survivor's pension is also paid when the injured person is gone missing and has, on that occasion, probably faced a life-threatening accident and it is not to be expected that the person in question was saved.

404. The married spouse of the injured is entitled to receive the spouse's pension. The right is extended to live-in partner of the injured who, at the moment of the death, lived permanently in the same household under marriage-like circumstances with the injured and with whom the injured person had or has a child or with whom the injured had contracted an agreement of mutual maintenance, certified by a notary public. The spouse's pension is payable also when the child of the spouses is born after the death of the injured person.

405. The child not yet 18 years at the moment of death of the injured is entitled to the orphan's pension. Moreover, the child of the injured, already 18 years of age, involved in full-time studies or at the time of the death of the injured parent, incapable of independent maintenance due to illness, defect or disability, will be entitled to receive the orphan's pension as long as these circumstances persist, but no longer than to his or her 25th birthday. The entitlement to the orphan's pensions is also extended to the child of the spouse entitled to the spouse's pension who was maintained by the injured at the time of death. The child always has the right to receive the orphan's pension after his or her own parent's death. However, the orphan's pension is paid simultaneously after the death of maximum two deceased parenting persons.

406. The funeral grant is EUR 4,830.

Chapter 7. Prevention of Occupational Diseases

407. The employers are generally responsible for occupational safety, thereby preventing the occurrence of accidents and occupational diseases. Likewise, the legislation on accident insurance (Workers' Compensation Insurance Act) aims at the prevention of accidents and occupational diseases, with the additional objective of shorter invalidity periods through rehabilitation. In part, the accident insurance premium policy is one means of attaining these objectives.

Chapter 8. Supplementary Benefits

408. The injured will be compensated for the indispensable travelling and accommodation expenses caused by the medical care. The injured will receive a basic-rate care allowance if he or she requires, due to the injury or disease, care, assistance, monitoring or guidance. If such need is regular or almost regular in some daily functions, the amount of the allowance payable will depend on the need. A blind person will receive the highest allowance during the two years of becoming blind and thereafter half of that sum.

409. The injured person will receive a clothing supplement if he or she needs to use for at least three months, as a result of the accident, a disability aid, support or bandage or other aid that is liable to cause the wear and tear of clothing. The injured who is unable to take care of the home after the accident will receive a reasonable compensation for the indispensable additional costs thus incurred, however, no longer for a year calculated from the accident. The injured will receive compensation for broken glasses, hearing aids, dentures, support bands and back braces as well as prosthetic limbs, joints and body parts.

410. The handicap benefits will be paid to the injured for the permanent overall handicap caused by the injury or disease resulting from the accident. The handicap benefit is not a compensation for the impaired working capacity following the accident, or the costs incurred for the need for care or assistance or other losses otherwise reimbursed. 'Overall handicap' refers to the impairment of the functional capacity as a result of the accident. The functional capacity is compared with that of a healthy peer of the same age.

411. A person with serious injuries will receive compensation for the additional costs incurred for service housing. The necessary and reasonable costs incurred for a disability aid will be compensated to a severely injured person who, due to the injury or disease, will have indispensable need of such an aid in order to cope with the usual daily functions. Compensation is payable for the necessary and reasonable costs incurred for the changes made to the permanent home as well as the disability aids and equipment in the home of a severely injured person who, due to the injury or disease, has an indispensable need for these measures in order to cope with the usual daily functions. Compensation is payable for interpretation services if the injured needs interpretation due to a severe visual, hearing or speech impairment caused by the accident.

Chapter 9. No-fault Insurance

412. In order to become operative in terms of compensation, the accident insurance does not require fault or negligence from the employer's part. The purpose is to compensate for the personal injuries faced by the employee at work. However, the Workers' Compensation Insurance Act contains a special provision regarding the employee's role in industrial accidents. Intent or gross negligence may lead to a decrease in the compensation.

Chapter 10. Civil Liability

413. In principle, the insurance under the Workers' Compensation Insurance Act does not release the employer from general civil liability. Therefore, the employee may claim damages for an injury not covered by the respective accident insurance. In these cases, the employer often also faces penal responsibility.

Chapter 11. Accumulation Rules

414. The system under the Workers' Compensation Insurance Act is primary and in situations of collision, other benefits under the social insurance are withdrawn. Since the compensations under the insurance system provided for in the legislation are relatively high, only rarely do the employees receive benefits for their injuries or occupational diseases from other systems. The motor liability insurance is the most common exception.

Part VII. Unemployment Security and Employment Services

Chapter 1. Provision of Work

415. The purpose of the public employment and business services is to promote the functioning of the labour market by ensuring that competent labour force is available and that jobseekers are offered possibilities to find work. Another objective is to promote new business operations and improve the operating conditions of companies and the quality of working life. The offer of public employment and business services includes labour exchange services, information and advice services, competence development services and business start-up and development services. The public employment and business services also include expert assessments related to the service process offered to individual customers as well as the supports and compensations under the respective law.

416. Public employment services must be guided by the principles of equality and neutrality. They must not be used to influence labour disputes and vice versa, labour disputes must not influence the employment services. Gender equality must also be promoted. With certain exceptions, employment services are offered free of charge.

§1. Labour Meditation

417. Employment services are offered to all. However, to be included in the scope of services, one has to register. The registration can take place as a jobseeker or an unemployed jobseeker. The status of an unemployed jobseeker is very similar to the status of a person who is entitled to unemployment security.

418. Employment services are provided either as self-service or personally to customers. Self-service is mainly available on the web. The information and advice services provide information on vacancies and job seeking, availability of and access to labour force, training options and other means to develop one's competences, labour market, sectors and professions, running one's own business as well as various other services, forms of support and benefits. If necessary, the customers are referred to the social welfare, healthcare or educational authorities or other institutions providing rehabilitation.

419. Registration as a jobseeker can be under a general status or one can register as an unemployed jobseeker. Registration and job seeking will lapse if the person so wishes, if they do not renew the jobseeker status or if they do not provide the necessary explanations, report the actions taken to implement the employability plan or do not subject themselves to the necessary examinations. It is a general obligation of the unemployed jobseeker to seek work and training.

420. The services include employment exchange whereby the aim is to put the jobseeker and employer in contact with each other on the basis of contractual freedom.

421. The jobseeker's interviews and employability plan are also part of the employment services. The employment authorities must interview the jobseeker within a given timeframe, and the employability plan must also be made within a set time frame. The starting point of the employability plan is constituted by the jobseeker's own objectives related to work and training, and it will also contain a reference to the services that might improve their employability. Their working capacity and state of health may also be ascertained. The employment authorities are liable to actively offer work and training and to organise the services and measures referred to in the employability plan. However, such services are offered within the framework of allocated finances, and therefore there is no subjective right to access the services.

422. The jobseeker is obliged to contribute to the drafting of the plan. The refusal to participate in the drafting will result in the loss of unemployment benefits for the period of sixty days. The waiting period will be fifteen days if the person fails to attend the meeting to draft or to revise the employability plan. The jobseeker must also comply with the employability plan. Jobseekers who fail to follow the employability plan through their own action will not be entitled to receive the unemployment benefits for sixty days. Valid reasons not to follow the plan are similar to those applied to the refusal to accept work.

423. Services promoting employability include expert assessments such as competence and professional skill charting, working capacity examinations and assessments, evaluations related to business entrepreneur potentials and to the promotion of integration as well as various other expert opinions and evaluations. Moreover, the services offered may include professional and career guidance to support individuals in their choices, professional development, finding a place in the labour market and in lifelong learning. Other measures include job-seeking coaching and work and training trials.

§2. VOCATIONAL TRAINING

I. General Vocational Training

424. In Finland, most of the vocational training is provided by schools and institutes of learning. The extensive network of vocational schools comprises the whole country, and the students continue their studies either after their basic education or the general secondary-level education. There are about 130 secondary-level vocational schools with about 320,000 students. Mostly, the studies take three years. The number of universities of applied sciences is twenty-four and their students number about 140,000. In addition, Finland has a comprehensive network of vocational schools and institutes for adults.

II. Labour Training

425. Employment authorities may organise labour policy-related training to improve an adult's professional skills, possibilities to find work or keep their old job and their preparedness to operate as a self-employed person as well as to promote the availability of professionally competent labour force and generation of new business operations.

426. Training for professional skills and preparedness and integration training are also within the framework of labour force training. In certain cases, basic education for adults can also be provided. In exceptional cases, the training provided can also aim at a university degree. During such training, the student will receive social assistance in the form of unemployment benefits in line with the Unemployment Security Act.

III. Promotion of Employability

427. The rehabilitative work measures are used to improve the open-market employability conditions of a person receiving labour market support or social assistance on the basis of long-lasting unemployment as well as to promote their possibilities to participate in training or other employability measures offered by the employment authorities.

428. This Act is applied for the drafting of the activation plan and organising of rehabilitative work for an unemployed young person less than 25 years of age, entitled to receive labour market support or receiving social assistance and also meeting certain criteria of the employability plan provided for earlier. The Act is also applied to long-term unemployed persons over 25 with an employability plan already made.

429. During the rehabilitative work activities, the labour market support, expense reimbursements and social assistance are paid in line with the general legislation on these benefits.

430. The activation plan related to the rehabilitative work activities is drafted by the employment authorities and the municipality in collaboration with the person in question. The employment authorities and the municipality are obliged to start drafting the activation plan when they become aware of a person meeting the criteria of a recipient of this type of service. The costs incurred by the municipalities for rehabilitative work activities are reimbursed to the local authorities from State funds.

431. The activation plan must include information on the individual's training and work history, an estimate of the impact of the previous measures to promote employability, an assessment of the materialisation of the employability plan and other plans related to the individual, as well as the measures to be taken. The measures may include offers of work, measures to promote employability, rehabilitative work, other social welfare services as well as healthcare, rehabilitation and training services. The offer of work and employability measures are primary.

432. The individual is obliged to participate in the drafting of the activation plan. Not attending the meeting to draft the activation plan and refusal to participate in the activation plan are deemed to correspond to a refusal defined in the Unemployment Security Act.

IV. Integration of Immigrants Through Employment

433. According to the Act on the Promotion of Immigrant Integration, the purpose of the operations is to support and promote integration and make it easier for immigrants to play an active role in the Finnish society. The Act is applied to those with a valid residence permit in Finland and to certain other immigration situations.

434. The integration measures and services constitute a part of basic municipal services and may also be part of the measures implemented in the framework of the services under the administration of the Ministry of Employment and the Economy. The immigrants are provided with basic information on the Finnish society as well as on their right and obligations in the employment sector and society at large. They will also be informed about the general services systems and measures to promote integration.

435. The integration plan is specific to an individual immigrant and contains the measures and services designed to support the individual's possibilities to learn enough Finnish or Swedish and other necessary skills and competences. In addition to language courses, the integration plan may cover the immigrant's own language teaching, instruction on the Finnish society, teaching of reading and writing or complementing their basic education as well as on integration training and other similar measures. An unemployed jobseeker immigrant registered with the employment authorities and normally also other immigrants are entitled to have a personalised immigration plan made. The plan is made in collaboration with the immigrant in question.

436. The employment authorities must agree with the immigrant on the services and other measures taken. In the case of underage immigrants, an integration plan is likewise made if, considering the young person's individual circumstances, there is a reason to do so. Underage immigrants arriving without a guardian will always have integration plans.

437. The municipal and employment authorities will agree on their own obligations and the immigrant is expected to follow the integration plan made. The implementation of the integration plan is subject to the financial appropriations available. Those refusing the implementation of the integration plan without a valid reason will face the same limitations resulting from refusals referred to in the Unemployment Security Act or the Social Assistance Act.

438. The integration support payable to immigrants takes the form of labour market support (*See* paragraphs 444–484) or social assistance (*See* paragraphs 629–640). The entitlement to these support forms is determined under the respective laws.

439. The municipality of residence must support integration through general services and by promoting internationalisation, democracy and equality as well as positive interaction. Municipal services must also be suitable for immigrants, and the municipality must organise immigrant services according to the needs emerging in the municipality. One municipality acting alone or several municipalities together must draft an immigration plan. At the national level, the government adopts the State immigration plan for four years at a time.

§3. Direct Work Provision

440. Pay subsidy is a support with a purpose of promoting the employment of an unemployed jobseeker. It is a form of support that is granted to the employer to cover the expenses incurred for pay. The purpose of the work arranged with the help of pay subsidy is to improve the unemployed jobseeker's professional competence and to help them becoming employed on the open labour market.

441. Pay subsidy can be granted if it is estimated that the employed person's productivity in the job offered would be lower due to shortcomings in competence and professional skills as a result of the duration of unemployment, durability or disease or similar reasons.

442. Depending on the length of preceding unemployment, the pay subsidy can account for 30%, 40% or 50% of the pay. In the case of disabled and sick persons, the pay subsidy is 50% if the respective handicap or disease causes the person's productivity to decrease permanently and significantly.

443. Support can also be granted for start-up business operations or in the form of reimbursement of expenses during labour policy measures, travel and accommodation expenses and transfers.

Chapter 2. Unemployment Benefit

444. The purpose of unemployment security is to safeguard the unemployed job-seeker's economic possibilities to seek employment and to improve the conditions of entering or returning to the labour market. The Finnish unemployment security is divided into two parts: the unemployment allowance is paid to a person with a permanent status in the labour market, with the subsistence based on paid employment, business operations or corresponding own work. The unemployment allowance is paid to persons who meet the work criterion. Membership in an unemployment fund is voluntary. An earnings-related allowance is paid to the members of an unemployment fund. People not organised in an unemployment fund will only receive the basic allowance.

445. Labour market support is paid to a jobseeker with no established status on the labour market or who has received the unemployment allowance for the maximum period.

446. Anyone receiving unemployment security has the right to receive the services mentioned in the employability plan as per the Act on Public Employment and Business Service. However, it is the beneficiary's obligation to actively seek work or training, to provide the authorities with information on their work history, competence, training and working capacity as well as to follow the employability plan made. If necessary, they must also seek and participate in services promoting employability.

447. The implementation of unemployment security is divided between the labour administration and the unemployment security administration. Labour policy issues are the competence of the Ministry of Employment and the Economy and the administration under its umbrella. In turn, unemployment security issues are covered by the Ministry of Social Affairs and Health as well as by the unemployment funds for their members and by the Social Insurance Institute Kela as far as the basic allowance and employment support are concerned.

§1. Field of Application

I. Territorial

448. Permanent residents of Finland are entitled to unemployment security, as well as individuals who have the right to receive it under international conventions, *see* 57–59.

II. Personal

449. To receive the unemployment allowance, the person in question must be 17 while the upper limit is 65 years. However, there are certain exceptions to the 65-year rule.

450. A person incapable of work is not entitled to the unemployment benefit. Under the Unemployment Allowances Act, 'disabled for work' refers to someone who is eligible for the sickness allowance under the Health Insurance Act or the national disability pension under the National Pensions Act or the benefit payable on the basis of full disability under another Act (usually the Employees Pensions Act). In particular circumstances, the recipient of the national disability pension may be eligible for unemployment benefits if the person in question has a severe visual or hearing or mobility handicap.

451. Unemployment security is not paid to anyone on old-age pension or receiving the parent's allowance or certain other social benefits. Persons receiving a salary or wages or similar compensation will not be eligible for unemployment benefits. If the person in question receives pay for the period of notice or an annual vacation, no unemployment benefit can be paid. Normally, certain severance payments also prevent the person from receiving unemployment benefits. This type of benefit is considered to be a preventive benefit and the quarantine period is calculated from the previous salary.

452. Certain social benefits will reduce the sum of the unemployment benefit. A disability pension paid from abroad as well as the amount of the pension to those with a severe visual, hearing or mobility handicap lower the unemployment benefit sum. However, unemployment security is not decreased by benefits that compensate for particular circumstances or are cost reimbursements by nature. Disability allowances, handicap benefits, housing allowances, child benefits and social assistance payments do not decrease the unemployment benefit sum.

453. If a jobseeker receives child home care allowance, the aggregate sum received by the jobseeker and the spouse in child home care allowance is deducted from the unemployment benefit.

454. Unemployment security is not payable during a labour dispute if the purpose of the action is to influence the interested person's work and pay conditions.

455. Adjusted unemployment can be paid to those in a part-time job. However, part-time work must not be a choice of the employee. The adjusted unemployment benefit can be paid if the person's daily or weekly working hours have been shortened due to a layoff or if the work has been prevented due to a labour dispute which does not relate to the individual's terms and conditions of work.

456. The unemployment allowance is granted either in the earnings-related or basic benefit form. The earnings-related unemployment allowance can be paid to those who have taken out a voluntary insurance at an unemployment fund. The unemployment funds are either employee funds or entrepreneur funds. A non-insured employee is covered by the basic unemployment benefit system.

457. In order to receive the allowance, the person must meet the work criterion. This means that the person must have worked at least for twenty-six calendar weeks during the immediately preceding twenty-eight months. For the self-employed, the criterion is defined as forty-eight months and fifteen of them as an entrepreneur. To receive the earnings-related allowance, the work criterion must be during the membership in the fund. The twenty-eight month period of accrual will be extended if the person in question is prevented, for a justified reason, from being at the disposal of the labour market. Such reasons may include disease, institutional care, rehabilitation, military or civil service, full-time studies, birth of a child and the caring for a child under 3 years of age.

458. Normally, the work criterion is only met with work performed in employment. However, tenured employment and work under the Seamen's Employment Contracts Act also meet the criterion. Work performed under an apprenticeship contract is normally deemed to meet the work criterion. Except for certain cases, the working hours in a calendar week must be at least eighteen hours.

459. The social security payments and tax withdrawals related to the work must have been made. The employer is responsible for making the withdrawals and respective payments. If the employer has failed to do this and the employee operates in bona fide, the failure to make the payments does not impact the accrual of working time required for the work criterion to be met.

460. The pay constituting the basis for the earnings-related allowance is calculated on the established pay received during the period preceding unemployment, with the person fulfilling the work criterion. The allowance related to seasonal work is calculated on the basis of the person's annual earnings. The earnings-related allowance of a self-employed person is calculated on the basis of the earned income used by the interested person when insuring themselves with the respective unemployment fund for the maximum aggregate of eighteen months prior to unemployment. However, earned income cannot exceed the amount adopted by the interested person as the basis of the pension under the Pensions Acts applicable to entrepreneurs or farmers.

461. The basic allowance and the earnings-related allowance are paid for the maximum of 500 days of unemployment in total. In certain cases, the allowance is paid for 400 or 300 days. The adjusted allowance is converted into full allowances, payable for five weekdays in a week. Therefore, the limit of 500 days of unemployment corresponds to about 100 weeks.

462. The period of allowances starts once the wage earner has again met the work criterion, and correspondingly, the self-employed person will start receiving the allowance when the respective criterion is met.

463. The purpose of labour market support is to ensure subsistence during the job-seeking period for jobseekers who are not entitled to receive unemployment allowance. The support is also there to promote the individual's possibilities to improve their potential to enter or return to the labour market. It can also be paid to persons who have received the unemployment benefit for the maximum period of time.

464. Another criterion for receiving labour market support is that the person is at the disposal of the labour market (*See* paragraph 473). The payment of the support starts only after a twenty-one week waiting period if the jobseeker does not fulfil the work criterion and has not completed any vocational training after the basic education or upper secondary school. The waiting period starts with registering as an unemployed jobseeker or from the end of the prescribed timeframe. When the person has after registering as a jobseeker been employed for five months in employment meeting the work criterion, or as a self-employed person or unemployed jobseeker or in employability services, the labour market support can be paid.

465. However, the right to labour market support may be withdrawn when the person in question has had it for 500 days if they, without a valid reason, refuse or resign from the work or is dismissed for a reason attributable to themselves from work or training or if they refuse to accept various employability measures.

§2. Amount of the Benefit

466. The full labour market support and the basic unemployment allowance per diem are of the same amount (EUR 32.40 in 2018). The person on an earnings-related allowance scheme will receive the full basic allowance plus 45% of the pay in excess of that sum. Once the pay is 105 times that of the basic allowance, the benefit will be 25% of the pay in excess of the basic allowance. The unemployed is required to show activeness during a sixty-five day period at a time. It the activeness criterion is not met, the support will be reduced by 4.65%. The unemployment allowance is paid for 300 days to those who have been in the labour market for less than three years and maximum 400 days to those who have worked for over three years. As concerns the unemployed who are over 58 years of age and have worked for longer than five years, the benefit can be paid for the maximum of 500 days (calculated on the basis of a five-day working week).

467. Parents with children are eligible for an increase in the benefit. The daily increase is EUR 5.23 for one child, EUR 7.68 in total for two children and EUR 9.90 in total for three or more children.

468. The labour market support is subject to means testing. Under this regime, the person's full labour market support calculated per month is diminished by 50% of the element of the income exceeding the allowance in euros. In other words, an income of EUR 1 will lead to a decrease of 50 cents in the labour market support.

The means testing of persons with liability to provide maintenance is less stringent, and they will have privileged income and a smaller decrease percentage. However, means testing is not applied if the person is participating in employability services. During the employability service period, the labour market support can be higher for the maximum of 200 days. The increase is EUR 4.74 a day. The labour market support payments do not have a time limit.

469. However, there are regulations covering the level of adjusted labour market support. The protected sum is EUR 300, meaning that the person can earn this gross sum in a month without the earnings impacting the amount of the unemployment allowance paid.

470. The unemployment security schemes include a waiting period of five working days.

§3. CONDITIONS

471. The unemployed jobseeker must look for full-time work. In certain cases, jobseekers looking for part-time employment may also receive unemployment benefits. 'Unemployed' refers to a person not in employment, nor in full-time self-employment or performing their own work. Students do not qualify as jobseekers. To become an unemployed jobseeker, one has to expressly register with the employment administration.

472. It is often difficult to draw the line between unemployment and entrepreneurial work, own work and study. The main rule is that the person is not entitled to receive unemployment benefits for the period in which they are self-employed on a full-time basis or involved in corresponding self-employed activities or work. The problem most often arises from the definition of the beginning and end of entrepreneurship or self-employment. In defining full-time studies, the criteria are mostly based on the objectives of the studies. If the objective is a degree completed in an institute of learning and the studies meet with the statutory scope defined in the law, the student is deemed to be a full-time student. If the place of study is other than the above, the scope of the curriculum, the involvement required by the studies and the person's possibilities to accept full-time work are taken into account.

473. To receive unemployment security, the person in question must be at the disposal of the labour market. The unemployed must not set any personal restrictions that prevent them from receiving the work offered on generally applied terms or from participating in suitable training. However, the jobseeker must be reserved reasonable time to make arrangements for child care and to solve any travelling difficulties or similar restrictions. Imposing restrictions which lead to resignation from work or abandoning training means that the person in question is no longer at the disposal of the labour market. If necessary, the person must prove that the self-imposed restrictions are no longer in force. There are separate provisions related, for example, to the impact of travelling abroad, military or civil service, imprisonment and hospital care or similar institutional care on the person being available for work.

474. During the three first months of unemployment, the unemployed jobseeker enjoys the so-called professional skills protection. During this period, the person may legitimately refuse work not corresponding to their specific professional skills. However, the professional skills protection is removed if the employment authorities assess that during the first three months of unemployment there is no work available to match the person's skills available in the commuting area.

475. Jobseekers who have resigned from work without any valid reason or have caused the termination of the employment through their own action will lose the right to the unemployment benefits for the period of ninety days. In certain cases, this period may be shorter.

476. A jobseeker refusing to accept work will not be entitled to receive the unemployment benefits for sixty days from the date of refusal. If the refusal is due to a valid reason, the right to unemployment security continues. Refusal to accept work may take place in a situation where the authorities specifically indicate work to the jobseeker matching their working capacity, with the pay corresponding to the collective agreement and the place of work not in a situation of labour dispute. In certain cases, the entitlement to unemployment benefits may be lost for a shorter period of time. Normally, jobseekers are obliged to accept work in their respective commuting area. It is also possible to refuse the work if the tasks offered are indecent or against the general morality or if the work is associated with evident threat of violence or health hazard or danger. Religious or ideological factors may also entitle to a valid refusal of work.

477. Moreover, the jobseeker may validly refuse to accept work if the daily commuting for a full-time job would be in excess of three hours and in part-time work two hours on average.

478. There are certain additional provisions regulating the refusal to accept work offered outside the commuting area. It is not possible to refuse work if the employment authorities assess that there are no employees living and available in the commuting area and if the work provides permanent income in a full-time employment. There is also the question of the jobseeker's and their family's home. For weighty personal reasons, it is always possible to refuse work outside the commuting area. Such reasons include the studies or schooling of the jobseeker, the spouse or the children at their locality of residence, the care of a close family member and certain corresponding situations.

479. In addition to the refusal to accept work, also the refusal to participate in training or leaving the training of one's own accord results in sanctions. In these situations, the person in question is not entitled to receive unemployment benefits for a period of sixty days. Valid reasons to refuse training are similar to those applied to the work offered. The training must be suitable for the person in question and it must be in line with the training plan or curriculum indicated in advance.

480. The sixty-day waiting period also ensues from refusing to accept or interrupting the use of employability services. Such services include trial work, job coaching and trial work combined with training.

481. If someone repeatedly refuses to accept work or to participate in training or it is otherwise evident that the unemployed is not willing to accept work, training or employability services, they will not be entitled to unemployment benefits until they have, for at least three months, worked in a job meeting with the working criteria or taken part in adult education of labour policy nature or been a full-time student in vocational training or studied for a university degree or upper secondary school leaving certificate.

482. The young under 25 years of age are subject to particular provisions. They cannot receive labour market support for the period of unemployment unless they have completed a post-secondary or post-matriculation vocational training providing them with professional skills. An exception to this are persons for whom no work, training or employability services have been found despite their active job-seeking efforts or training pursuits.

483. The requirement of the own active initiative of such young persons is further emphasised by the fact that the young without vocational training are not entitled to receive labour market support if they have, without justified reasons, refused or resigned or have been dismissed from work or suitable training during which their subsistence has been reasonably secured. A person under 25 can regain the right to receive labour market support if they have completed a training or been working so that they meet the work criterion or been in on-the-job training, trial work or labour policy-related adult education for at least five months.

484. The young are expected to seek training in places where they meet the admittance criteria. They must also meet the requirements of seeking training agreed upon in the employability plan.

§4. Job Alternation Leave

485. The purpose of job alternation leave is to use a short-term absence to promote the employee's coping with the work, at the same time improving a jobseeker's employability through temporary work experience. The respective Act is applied to employees and tenured officials. Normally, the Act is not applicable to self-employed persons.

486. 'Job alternation leave' refers to an arrangement where the employee makes an agreement with the employer and will be temporarily released from the tasks under the employment contract and where the employer simultaneously undertakes to employ an unemployed jobseeker.

487. The requirement for the job alternation arrangement is that entitled to receive the old-age pension no earlier than after three years the employee has a career of at least twenty years, or if job alternation compensation has already been paid to the employee at an earlier stage, the employee has worked for five years after such a period. Moreover, immediately prior to the job alternation leave, the employment must have lasted uninterruptedly for at least thirteen months. The job alternation leave can last from 100 to 180 calendar days.

488. The substitute hired for the job must be an unemployed jobseeker, out of work for at least ninety calendar days during the fourteen months preceding the substitute job, or a recently graduated person of less than 30 years, or someone under 25 or over 55. The substitute cannot be a student. The working hours of the substitute must be those of the employee on job alternation leave.

489. The respective Act also contains provisions on the premature end of the job alternation leave, temporary return to work, the end of employment of the substitute as well as the ordinary employee's right to reassume the work.

490. During the job alternation leave, the person on leave has the right to receive a compensation. The full amount of the compensation is 70% of the unemployment allowance the individual would be entitled to in case of unemployment. In certain cases, it may be higher. Certain other benefits lower the job alternation compensation.

Part VIII. Pensions

491. The general purpose of pension security is to safeguard the subsistence of individuals faced with certain risks of life. Pensions ensure a reasonable income security in view of old age and disability for work. Pensions are also used as an income security during rehabilitation, in which case the objective is to prevent invalidity or help the individual to regain their working capacity. Pensions also provide income security for the surviving spouse and underage children of a deceased person.

492. The Finnish pension security can be categorised in many ways. One way is to distinguish national old-age pensions from statutory employee pensions. The purpose of the national pension system is to provide basic income security during old age and invalidity as well as after the loss of a provider and the spouse. The national pension system also includes the concept of 'guarantee pension' which secures a certain level of pensions as well as the pensioner's housing allowance and basic-rate care allowance (*See* paragraphs 619, 625–628). In turn, the purpose of the statutory employee pension system is to ensure a reasonable income when the inherent risk materialises, in other words during old age and invalidity as well as after the loss of the spouse and provider.

493. Another way to break up the Finnish pension security is to look at different kinds of pensions and divide them into old-age pensions, invalidity pensions and survivors' pensions. All of the above are paid out both in the form of employee pensions and national pensions or a combination of both. The basic rationale of the old-age pension is to secure the subsistence of those who have reached a certain age. The invalidity pension secures subsistence when an individual is unfit for work while survivors' pensions compensate for the loss of income of the surviving spouse and underage children. The national pension secures a basic subsistence while the employees' pension compensates for the loss of income.

494. The third way to analyse the pension system is based on the criteria of access to the type of pension. The employees' pension accumulates on the basis of work. The individuals' earnings-related pension accumulates as they receive pay in employment or tenured position, or income as a self-employed person. The invalidity pension is also associated with the so-called protected pensionable service. The concept means that the time from the beginning of invalidity until the start of the old-age pension is included in the period entitling one to the pension. The national pension system is based on residence in Finland and the pension accumulates on the basis of the years of residence. The old-age pension and the invalidity pension accumulate on the basis of personal residence while the survivors' pension element in the national pension system looks at the time of residence of the deceased and the beneficiary in Finland.

495. The fourth type of division could be the way in which the benefits are funded (*See* paragraphs 106, 111, 114, 117, 118, 121–141, 154–157 and 160). The employee pensions are funded through the earnings-related employee pension premiums paid by the employers and employees or, as the case might be, by a self-employed person. The employee pension system also includes elements funded by tax money. The national pension is financed through the State budget.

496. The Finnish employee pension system underwent a complete reshuffle as of 1 January 2005. The above text reflects this reform. The calculation of pensions started from scratch. The pensions accrued by the end of 2004 were recalculated to the level of the end of 2004 and they were regarded to constitute so-called vested pensions. In a contingency, these pensions are combined with the pensions earned during the new legislation.

497. Starting from the year 2017, the Finnish pension system has been under reform with the objective of ensuring its sustainability. The most significant change is the gradual increase of the general pensionable age to reflect the life expectancy of the people.

498. Athletes are covered by a particular pension system which is based on a certain minimum income earned in sports. The old-age security includes an old-age insurance paid as from the age of 65. The security is arranged through an insurance policy granted by an insurance company.

Chapter 1. Pensions for Wage Earners

§1. OLD-AGE PENSION

I. Beneficiaries

A. *Territorial Field of Application*

499. Persons covered by pension insurance are those working in Finland under the Employees Pensions Act, Seamen's Pensions Act, Public Sector Pensions Act or certain minor Act covering the public sector employees.

500. Employees working abroad are covered by the Finnish legislation as per the EU regulations or conventions on social security if the scope of application of the law is otherwise met. The Act will also be applied to work performed by the employee as an expat employee in a third country not applying the EU social security legislation or conventions, provided that the employee is working either for the Finnish employer sending him or her abroad or for a foreign company which is part of the same financial entity (group of companies), the employee's employment relationship with the Finnish company continues after the foreign assignment and the employee is covered by the Finnish social security legislation when leaving Finland for the assignment. There are certain exceptions related to the work abroad.

B. *Personal Field of Application*

501. See 57–59.

II. Conditions

502. The employees in a private sector employment are insured in compliance with the Employees Pensions Act. The Act covers all private sector work, with the exception of the contracts of service under the Seamen's Pensions Act or the work of self-employed persons and athletes. The self-employed persons are insured under the Self-Employed Persons Pensions Act while the farmers are covered by the Farmers Pensions Act. Those employed by a municipality, State, Evangelical-Lutheran Church or Kela are insured under Public Sector Pensions Act. In addition, there are certain minor public sector pension systems, such as the pension schemes of the Orthodox Church, the Bank of Finland and the Provincial Government of Åland.

503. Those in an employment are insured under the Employees Pensions Act. In the context of Labour Law, this is a so-called basic relationship with the following distinctive features: (1) work is performed under a contract; (2) a salary or wages or other remuneration is paid for the work; and (3) the work is performed under the direction and control of the employer. In certain situations it may be difficult to distinguish self-employed persons from employees if the only factor is to determine the factual rate of direction and control exercised by the employer. Other distinguishing factors may include questions whether the commitment to work is personal, whose tools are used, to what extent the person is entitled to decide on the mode of work and whether the contract comprises the entrepreneurial risk.

504. The Employees Pensions Act must be applied to and insurance taken for all employees at the private employer's service in Finland, between 17 and 68 years of age and earnings amounting to at least EUR 58.29 in a month (year 2018). Gradually, the upper limit will be 70 years for those born in 1962 or later. Retired employees must also be insured. The insurance obligation covers all persons at the employer's service, also those with executive duties. For example, the Managing Director of a limited liability company must be insured under the Employees Pensions Act. The exceptions are only constituted by certain executives in limited liability companies who are also shareholders in the said company. Their ownership share has a bearing on whether they are considered paid employees or entrepreneurs. In these cases, also the ownership shares of family members may have importance bearing for the question. The conclusive factor is the degree of their factual decisive powers.

505. A crucial rule of insurance is that it is normally taken in the country where work is performed. The nationality of the employee is not important. International conventions cause certain exceptions to apply, for example, to diplomats. Correspondingly, the EU legislation results in certain situations where the status of a seconded worker sent to another country is different from the status of an employee posted to Finland.

506. The employer is obliged to take out insurance for the employees. Pension security must be arranged for no later than during the month following the start of payroll payments. The employer chooses the insurance company and can opt to use several companies. The employee pension institution cannot refuse underwriting a pension since the employee pension insurance is the employer's statutory obligation. The general supervisory body in pension insurance issues is the Finnish Centre for Pensions. It may take out the pension insurance at the employer's cost if the employer ignores the admonition and neglects the obligation to take out insurance for the employee. The ensuing sanction may be an increased premium.

507. To be able to follow the accumulation of their pensions, the employees are provided with extracts of their pension schemes every three years or upon request. The employee can report any shortcomings or mistakes to the pension institution, and any undisputed mistakes noted must be rectified. The employee dissatisfied with the decision taken by the pension institution can lodge a complaint with the Finnish Centre for Pensions.

508. The main rule of insuring according to the Seamen's Pensions Act is that the Act is applied to an employee working on board a Finnish merchant ship as referred to in the Seafarers' Employment Contracts Act. The Act does not apply to independent entrepreneurs because they are not in an employment as per the Seafarers' Employment Contracts Act; they will be insured according to the Self-Employed Persons Pensions Act. To be in an employment under the Seafarers' Employment Contracts Act, the employee must be at least 16 years of age. The nationality of the employee does not play a role. All employees on board the ship are covered by the Seamen's Pensions Act, with certain exceptions applicable to vessels that have exceptional terms of work.

509. Municipal employees and officeholders are insured under the Public Sector Pensions Act. According to the law, municipalities and consortia of municipalities are direct member corporations of the pension insurance company Keva and therefore employers are liable to provide local pension security. Municipalities and their consortia have to be members of Keva. Upon application, associations can also become Keva's member corporations if their affiliates are exclusively municipalities or their consortia. Moreover, limited liability companies fully owned by Keva members can also become members. It is also sufficient that the corporation in question is a limited liability company or a foundation controlled by one or several municipalities or consortia of municipalities, implementing statutory tasks imposed on municipalities or operations directly serving such tasks, or the majority of the employees of which were, before the incorporation of the limited liability company or the foundation, within the scope of application of the Local Government Employees' Pensions Act. This provision aims at safeguarding the status of the employees in a situation where the municipality privatises its operations or transfers employees to a new company. If the said companies or foundations do not become members of Keva, they have to insure the employees under the Employees Pensions Act.

510. The Public Sector Pensions Act covers the insurance of State employees with a tenured office or employment. By virtue of Act, the pension security also covers certain other employee groups.

511. The Public Sector Pensions Act also covers the insurance of persons employed by Parliament. However, pensions of members of Parliament and ministers are regulated by separate legislation although the benefits enjoyed by the members of Parliament correspond largely to those provided by the Public Sector Pensions Act The scope of application of the Public Sector Pensions Act has also been adjusted to those employed by the European Union because there could otherwise be borderline situations that might be difficult to manage.

512. Reference was made above to other pensions based on a public service relationship. In practice, these pension systems correspond to the system under the Public Sector Pensions Act.

513. The old-age pension under a private pension system (Employees Pensions Act, Self-Employed Persons Pensions Act, Farmers Pensions Act and Seamen's Pensions Act) starts at 63 to 68 years of age. The pension starts to run at the choice of the person in question. The pensionable age of those born after 1954 is increased by three months until their 65th year. Those born in 1965 will be covered by a new procedure whereby the pensionable age increases (or decreases) in line with the change in the general age of the population. The upper limit of the insurance obligation imposed on the employers will increase to 70 years of age by the year 2024. The start of the pension can be postponed when the lowest pensionable age has been reached, and in that case the pension will be increased by 0.4% for each month of postponement.

514. Seamen's pension contains certain exceptions.

515. For those employed in municipal service covered by the Public Sector Pensions Act, the old-age pension starts at the age of 63–68 years, and the increase follows the system applicable to the private sector. Due to particular changes made to the local government pension system in the 1990s, there are, however, a significant number of municipal employees whose old-age retirement time is different from the above during a certain transitional period. These changes have had a bearing on both the retirement age and the amount of the pension. Within the old local government system, the employees have also had the right to choose the retirement age in connection with the legislative changes.

516. The State employees who retire are entitled to the pensions according to the same rules applicable to other groups. Compared to the municipal employees, the State employees face even more exceptions based on earlier pensions systems. The State employees have also been able to choose their previous, lower retirement age. A particular case within the State pensions system is the lower retirement ages applied to the military professions in Defence Forces and Frontier Guard.

517. The old-age pension can be payable as from the beginning of the month following the person's 62nd birthday, at the rate of either 25% or 50% of the whole. In this case, the amount of the pension is cut by 0.4% each month of anticipation in relation to the person's first pensionable age. The limit of 62 years will be increased in the 2020s. The partial anticipated old-age pension cannot be granted if the person in question already receives another work-based pension. The person receiving the partial anticipated old-age pension may work according to his or her choice.

518. The pension system also includes the option of an 'employment career' pension for those who have reached 63 years of age. The conditions for receiving this pension include a heavy physical work, diminished working capacity and weaker working conditions.

519. The partial anticipated old-age pension and employment career pension payable under the public sector pension scheme are very similar to those applicable to private sector employees. Any differences are mainly due to the varying transition systems derived from the old public sector pension rules.

III. Pension calculation

520. The pension under the Employees Pensions Act accumulates from three sources. The main element of accumulation is the work-related earnings of the insured. In addition, certain benefits obtained during periods of no pay as well as the disability pension under the employee pension legislation also increase the pension.

521. The pension starts to accumulate on the work performed by the employee after 17 years of age. The pension grows by 1.5% of the annual income.

522. The pension accrues as long as the employer has the insurance obligation. (*See* paragraph 513)

523. The earnings from work performed during disability pension or other pensions accumulate the pension by 1.5% a year. However, certain limits are imposed on the earnings during disability pension, and if these limits are exceeded, the need for disability pension will be verified. The new pension accrued during disability pension will be converted into old-age pension at the same time as the disability pension, provided that the working ends or has already ended.

524. If the person's disability pension continues until the pensionable age, the pension is automatically converted into an old-age pension of the same amount, and the new pension potentially accrued during the disability pension period is added to the old-age pension. If the disability pension expires before the pensionable age, the rate of accrual of pension is 1.5% during the disability pension period until the last month of the period. In disability pension, the sum used as the basis of accrual is constituted by the future earnings also used for the disability pension quantification. If no projected pension right is applied to the employee, the disability pension does not accumulate new pension.

525. The work-related earnings taken as the basis of pension calculations is normal pay or other remuneration paid or agreed to be paid as a compensation for the work. However, the minimum amount of pay that will accumulate the pension is EUR 58.27 per month (year 2018). The premium of the employee pension insurance is paid annually. Thus, the Finnish system is based on a defined benefit pension scheme, and the premium collected annually corresponds to the needs of the pension system.

526. The employee pension is also accumulating during certain periods with earnings-related benefits. However, the person must have earned certain minimum sums before the contingency. The rate of accrual during the periods without pay is 1.5% of the benefit paid to the employee.

527. The following accrue the pension: parental allowances, earnings-related unemployment allowance and sickness allowance, the allowance payable for industrial accidents under the Workers' Compensation Insurance Act or the Compensation for Military Injuries Act as well as the compensation for loss or earnings paid in a traffic accident case as well as certain other benefits. Certain rehabilitation benefits and other compensations for loss of earnings also normally accumulate the employee pension.

528. Likewise, the period of home care of a child aged under 3 years and the period of study also accumulate the pension. The pension benefit accrues at the time of study provided that the student graduates. Interrupted studies do not give rise to pension. The pension accrues for a certain maximum number of years determined on the statutory length of the programme for the degree. The sum constituting the accrual basis for parental leave for the care of a child aged under 3 years and the studies is EUR 728.34 per month (2018).

529. In the local government pension system, the pension sum accrues in the same way as in the employee pension system. There are some exceptions resulting from previous legislation. State pensions accrue according to the same rules applied to private pensions, with certain exceptions resulting from old pension systems.

530. The amount of the old-age pension is the pensions accrued in each year, adjusted to the retirement level using a pay coefficient. The pay coefficient is based on the annual changes in the income and consumer price indexes. Moreover, the pension security is adapted to the life expectancy so that the capital value of the pension is adjusted according to the longer or shorter average length of life. For this purpose, the length-of-life coefficient is determined for each age cohort at 62. The length-of-life coefficient is based on average mortality statistics for five years. At the population level, a longer length of life means lower pension amounts while a shorter length of life makes pensions grow. The pension quantification can roughly be summarised as given below.

531. Pension = annual work-related earnings (adjusted with the pay index) x accrual percentage tied to age. Then the annual pension accruals obtained will be totalled and multiplied by the length-of-life coefficient determined on the basis of the year of birth.

532. In the payment phase, the pensions will be adjusted annually with the employee pension index, starting from the beginning of each year. The employee pension index is calculated using the annual change of the income index and the consumer price index on the third quarter of the calendar year. In the employee pension index, the weight of the price level change is about 0.8 while that of the pay level is 0.2.

533. The public sector pensions are determined in line with the same provisions applied to the pension under the Employees Pensions Act.

534. The partial anticipated old-age pension is based on the pension sum accrued by the beginning of the year in which the pension starts. The employee can choose between the 25% and 50% rate. The pension is reduced by 0.4% for each anticipated month of retirement until the first possible retirement age. The amount of the partial anticipated old-age pension is calculated using the same criteria applicable to other pension systems.

535. The pensions are augmented by the child increase (EUR 21.93 in month year 2018) if the pensioner's or the spouse's child of age under 16 lives in the same household. The child increase expires when the criteria are no longer met.

§2. Survivors Pension

I. Beneficiaries

536. The purpose of the survivors' pension under the Employees Pensions Act is to secure the subsistence of deceased person's surviving spouse, children, the spouses' joint and the survivor's children, ex-spouse as well as the surviving partner of a registered partnership. The survivors' pension is paid out of the pension or pension rights accumulated in the name of the deceased.

537. In certain cases the ex-spouse of the deceased may receive the survivor's pension. The precondition is that at the time of death the deceased was obliged to pay the ex-spouse alimony at certain intervals.

538. In a registered partnership, the surviving partner has the right to the survivor's pension under similar conditions applied to married spouses.

539. In the public sector pension system, the criteria applied to the survivor's pension are similar.

II. Conditions

540. Children under 18 at the time of the death of the deceased will be entitled to this pension after the deceased. This rule applies to the child of the deceased or the surviving spouse, living and sharing the same household with the surviving spouse and the deceased when alive. 'Child' also refers to an adopted child and a child to whom the deceased was liable to pay child maintenance. The children of the surviving partner in a registered partnership are also entitled to the child's pension if the child lived together with the surviving partner and the deceased at the time of the death.

541. The survivor's pension is paid after the decease of the spouse if the marriage between the two has been contracted before the deceased was 65 years of age and the survivor has or has had a child with the deceased. In cases where the spouses had no children but the marriage was contracted before the deceased was 65 and the survivor was 50, the marriage had continued for at least five years before the death of the deceased and the spouse was at least 50 at the time of death of the deceased or had been on disability pension for at least three years, the survivor is entitled to the pension.

542. The survivor pension right expires if the survivor contracts new matrimony before turning 50. The child's pension right expires at the age of 18 or when they are adopted in a family other than that of the deceased person's survivor or the new spouse of the survivor.

III. Calculation

543. The survivors' pension under the Employees Pensions Act is based on the pension which the deceased received or would have received. In other words, the basis is the deceased person's old-age pension or full disability pension. If the deceased was not retired at the time of death, the survivors' pension is calculated using the same method applied if the pension had become entitled to a full disability pension on the day of death. The aggregate amount of the survivors' pension paid to the surviving spouse and children cannot exceed the amount of the pension of the deceased.

544. The payment of the child's pension is independent of the pension payments to the surviving spouse, if any. The child's pension amount depends on the number of children entitled to the pension payments. Correspondingly, the amount of the survivor's pension is determined on the basis of the number of eventual children entitled to the pension payments. The ex-spouse's right to receive the survivors' pension also reduces the sum of the surviving spouse's pension. Furthermore, the surviving spouse's own pensions impact the survivors' pension, and the impacting factors include the pension currently paid or the calculatory pension. However, the surviving spouse's pension is free from deductions if the survivor has a child under 18 entitled to receive the survivors' pension, living with the survivor and the deceased at the time of death of the latter. Even if there are not underage children, the survivor will receive the survivor's pension for the first six months following the death of the deceased if the survivor is under 65 and does not receive employee pension. When the child becomes 18, the surviving spouse's pension is impacted, although this takes place only when the youngest child is 18. The survivors' pensions under other employee pension systems follow the provisions of the Employees Pensions Act.

Chapter 2. Pensions for the Self-employed

§1. Old-Age Pensions

545. According to the Self-Employed Persons Pensions Act, a self-employed person residing and operating in Finland is obliged to take out the pension insurance. 'Self-employed person' refers to an individual engaged in gainful work without having an employment contract or tenured position. The self-employed person must work in the company and therefore the mere ownership of a company does not provide the possibility nor impose an obligation of insurance. The insurance obligation starts at 18 and ends at the expiry of the insurance obligation (*See* paragraph 513). In addition, the business operations must run for at least four months and the annual value of the work contribution must be at least EUR 7,656.26 (in 2018). Earning less than above or despite being on an old-age pension, the person can be insured but it would then be a case of voluntary insurance. Family members can also be self-employed persons in the same company as long as each of them meets the criteria.

546. The insurance obligation also applies to the executive shareholders mentioned above in connection with the Employees Pensions Act if they own a determined share of the company alone or together with the family members. The responsibilities of the Finnish Centre for Pensions under the Self-Employed Persons Pensions Act are the same as under the Employees Pensions Act.

547. Farmers are insured under the Farmers Pensions Act. This Act covers those engaged in farming, fishers and reindeer herders, their family members and spouses and certain other persons engaged, together with the entrepreneur, in the said farming occupations. The insurance can also be taken under the Farmers Pensions Act on the auxiliary operation in which such persons are engaged in unless it constitutes a separate business of another company. The insurance obligation starts at 18 and ends at the expiry of the insurance obligation (*See* paragraph 513). The Farmers Pensions Act is also the legislation that applies to the insurance of scholars and artists on grants.

548. A further criterion for being covered by this pension insurance scheme is that the farming operations continue uninterruptedly for at least four months. The farm must also meet certain requirements imposed on the farm size and the value of the work contribution, and the individual must not be on old-age pension under the Pensions Acts.

549. The insurance obligation applicable to farmer-entrepreneurs is not associated with ownership but with a factual contribution to the work at the farm. Therefore, the arable land causing the obligation to insure can be leasehold property.

550. If both spouses participate in the farming operations and meet the other insurance criteria, they will be covered by the pension system under the Farmers Pensions Act. Special provisions apply to other family members.

551. The requirement imposed both on farmers and recipients of grants is that the income or grant is at least EUR 3,828.13 (2018). The persons must work in Finland uninterruptedly for at least four months.

552. The self-employed person's old-age pension under the Self-Employment Persons Pensions Act is determined under the same rules that of the employees. However, the self-employed person does not need to wind up the business to obtain the old-age pension. The total earnings-related income constituting the basis of the pension is calculated on the basis of annual earnings, in turn based on earnings adopted and notified by the self-employed person. However, the system contains certain flexible points due to the nature of the business operations. The basis of the Farmers Pensions Act is also the total earned income, calculated and determined in the same way as those of the self-employed persons. However, the farmers do not enjoy any flexibility in these matters (*See* paragraphs 137 and 138).

553. The self-employed person's partial anticipated old-age pension is granted at the choice of the person in question either at the rate of 25% or 50% of the final payable pension amount

554. Under the Farmers Pensions Act, the partial anticipated old-age pension criteria are very similar to those under the Self-Employed Persons Pensions Act.

555. The farmers may receive income support if they wind up their business before retirement. The aim is to reform the agricultural production structure. The principles of this system are in line with the EU regulations on agricultural systems. The system may be based on a change of generation, in which case the farmer passes the operations over to a successor. However, the system can also be based on the farmer ceding the farming business to an outsider involved in farming. This system is applied to agriculture and reindeer herding.

§2. Survivors' Pension

556. The survivors' pension payable to the family members of self-employed persons or farmers corresponds to the schemes under other pension systems.

Chapter 3. Disability Pensions

557. All parts of the Finnish pension system include a disability pension element to cater for long-term disability situations. The structure, financing, accumulation and other elements of the disability pension are very similar to the model of the old-age pension. The disability pension is versatile in form: it includes the right to have vocational rehabilitation, temporary rehabilitation assistance and disability pension, and all of these in full or partial form.

558. Efforts are made to prevent situations where people end up on disability pension, the motivation for this being based both on the expenditure incurred by the pension system and the public economy as well as on human considerations. This is the reason for providing rehabilitation that will prevent the disability pension or postpone its need. One example of this is vocational rehabilitation. Before granting the disability pension, the pension institute must ensure that the employee's chances of benefiting from rehabilitation have been investigated.

559. In the employee pension system, vocational rehabilitation is available to those under 63 years of age with a diagnosed disease, defect or injury that may cause a probable risk of disability for work. The employee must have had EUR 17,480.28 (year 2018) of annual earnings during the preceding five calendar years but no right to have rehabilitation under an accident insurance or motor liability insurance.

560. The disease, defect or injury causing the probable risk of disability must be real. This is based on an estimate according to which the person would probably become unfit for work in about five years without vocational rehabilitation measures and would then be eligible for the disability pension. When assessing the purposefulness of the rehabilitation, the person's age, profession, earlier activities and certain employment-related factors are taken into account. The core element in the assessment is to establish whether the rehabilitation would probably improve or restore the person's working capacity.

561. Before the rehabilitation starts, the employee must have a rehabilitation plan. It is normally made in collaboration with the employment authorities or the rehabilitation service providers. The aim is to identify a work or profession in which the individual could operate and which would correspond to their current profession or earlier work experience. The rehabilitation plan includes the measures designed for vocational rehabilitation.

562. The vocational rehabilitation supported by the employee pension institutes may include all methods available to promote the rehabilitation of the person in question. Normally, co-operation is also sought with the workplace of the person and, for example, suitable tasks and duties are looked for at the workplace.

563. The person in rehabilitation may also receive vocational training leading to a new profession. The methods associated with vocational qualifications can be used but general education is normally not an option. Business subsidies can be granted if the person wishes to start or continue an enterprise. The subsidies can be in the form of allowances or loans. Support can also be provided for the acquisition of different kinds of aids.

564. During vocational rehabilitation, the rehabilitee may receive rehabilitation assistance or allowance. The amount of the rehabilitation allowance is based on disability pension which is increased by 33% during the period of rehabilitation. The disability pension can also be increased similarly if the individual – while on this pension – participates in rehabilitation. The rehabilitation allowance can also be reduced if the person in question is partially disabled.

565. The disability pension under the Employees Pensions Act can be granted for an undetermined or determined period of time. If it is for a determined period of time, it is called cash rehabilitation benefit. The disability pension, be it for a determined or an undetermined period of time, can be granted for full or partial disability.

566. The full disability pension normally starts when the period of primary benefits under the Health Insurance Act has expired. This period corresponds to the first 150 days of allowance, followed by four or five calendar months, adding up to the total period of about a year.

567. The payment of partial disability pension starts from the beginning of the month following the start of disability. This benefit does not necessarily have a link to the allowance under the Health Insurance Act.

568. The disability pension is not granted to persons who have reached the pensionable age or for those who would reach this age limit during the sickness allowance payment period. In these cases, they would receive the old-age pension instead of the disability pension.

569. The disability pension can be discontinued at the application of the employee or initiative of the pension institute, if the person in question no longer meets the pension criteria. The grounds for suspension include the employee's work and the temporary increase in work-related earnings by over 60% of the established average earnings of the employee prior to the beginning of the disability period. The reason for discontinuation of the pension may also be a refusal, without acceptable reason, by the person in question to subject themselves to examinations ordered or rehabilitation and training arranged by the pension institute.

570. If the individual no longer meets the criteria of the disability pension, the respective payments and the pension will be discontinued. The cash rehabilitation benefit, i.e. the temporary disability pension, will expire at the end of the respective timeframe. If the disability situation continues, the person involved can send a new application for the disability pension. When the recipient of the disability pension reaches the pensionable age, he or she can convert the pension into the old-age pension.

571. Disability pension can be paid to a person of at least 17 years of age who has not reached the pensionable age. Moreover, the person in question must have a medically diagnosed disease, defect or injury that will cause disability that lasts for at least one year. In addition of the assessment of person's fitness for work, their training, work experience, age and social aspects are considered, including any possible impairment in the capacity for work. The starting point in the assessment of the impaired working capacity is a statement by the attending physician, normally also containing a therapy or rehabilitation plan. However, the statement alone does not provide the right to the disability pension; other aspects considered include the person's remaining functional capacity in view of coping with the work. It is a question of the individual's remaining capacity to earn an income.

572. The disability pension can be granted as a full or a partial pension. A full pension will be granted to those whose working capacity in view of earning an income is permanently impaired to the degree of 3/5. If the loss of the working capacity is deemed permanent and the working capacity can probably not be regained, the disability pension will be granted until further notice. Partial disability pension will be given to one whose working capacity is permanently impaired by at least 2/5. In this case the pension will be granted until further notice.

573. If the working capacity is impaired for a determined period for at least a year, the disability pension can be paid out in the form of cash rehabilitation benefit. The objective is the return to active employment. The criteria for obtaining the cash rehabilitation benefit are the same applied to the disability pension. The individual can return temporarily to work in which case the pension is interrupted or put on hold.

574. In the public sector pension system, the disability pension criteria are somewhat different from those in the private sector, albeit the basic principles are the same. The exceptions in the public sector pensions are a result of the profession-specific and private anticipated early retirement schemes previously included in these systems.

575. The disability pension included in the employee pensions system is calculated using the same method as in the old-age pension. Moreover, the disability pensions include the so-called projected pension.

576. The projected pension element associated with the disability pension is calculated as of the beginning of the year in which the person in question became unfit for work until the end of the calendar year in which the person meets the pensionable age criterion. The purpose of the projected pension is to compensate for the element of the pension not accrued due to the disability. The protected pension is calculated on the basis of the work-related earnings and the earnings constituting the basis for benefits for the time without pay which the employee has had during the five calendar years preceding the year of the contingency (review period). The protected pension and benefits are looked at on using the same criteria used for the earning times. Certain benefits paid for the periods without pay, not accruing old-age pension, are also taken into account. However, the protected pension cannot be obtained merely on the basis of periods without pay but the review period must always include pension-accruing work-related earnings.

577. These calculations come with certain exceptions. They are related, among other things, to the year of beginning of the disability, the impact of childcare time on the review period as well as the calculations on the protected period of a young person unfit for work.

578. The projected pension accrues the pension by 1.5% from the time of the contingency to the reaching of the lowest pensionable age. If the person receives a partial disability pension or partial cash rehabilitation benefits, the amount will be half of the full disability pension.

579. For a young person who has become unfit for work, the disability pension will be augmented with a one-off increase starting from the calendar year by which the pension has been paid for five years. This increase aims at ensuring a maintained level of the pension, considering also the fact that people normally enjoy earnings with an upward trend. The increase is determined on the basis of the age of the beneficiary at the time of the increase. The highest rate of increase is 25%, applicable to persons between 23 and 31. The rate of increase diminishes year by year down by 1% and ends by 55 years of age.

580. The disability pension under other pension systems is determined using the principles provided for in the Employees Pensions Act.

Chapter 4. Guaranteed Income for Old Persons

581. The general security for old age is the national old-age pension system that includes most of the pension elements envisaged by the employees' and self-employed persons' pension systems. The national old-age pension and associated guarantee pension are designed for persons who have not been employed for various reasons, such as their disability. The reasons for such non-participation in the workforce do not play a role.

582. To obtain the national pension, a person must live in Finland. Those residing in the country are entitled to the pension. An additional prerequisite applicable to the survivors' pension is that the deceased was living in Finland at the time of death. The pension can be paid to a person living in a country other than Finland if they are covered by the Regulation (EC) No 883/2004 of the European Parliament and of the Council on the coordination of social security systems.

583. In the regular national pension old-age pension system, the pension payments start at the age 65. For those born after 1965, the old-age pension under the national pension scheme is tied to the personal pensionable age as per the Employee Pensions Act. The old-age pension under the national pension system can start earlier than this. Anticipated payment decreases the level of the pension permanently by 0.4% per each month of anticipation. Correspondingly, postponing the pension increases the pension by 0.4% per month. Those born in 1962 or later no longer have the change to apply for the old-age pension under the national pension scheme.

584. The national pension is 'earned' through residence in Finland. The amount of the pension is influenced by the time of residence in Finland. The period taken into consideration is the time the person has lived in Finland between 16 and 65 years of age. If that time is less than 80% of the years between 16 and 65, a proportional coefficient is applied. In practice, this means more or less that each year out of 40 years that the person has not lived in Finland will diminish the national pension by 1/40.

585. The national pension system does not include any partial anticipated old-age pension or employment career pension options.

586. Under the national pension system, the disabled persons aged 16 to the reaching of their earliest pensionable age are entitled to the disability pension. Persons unable to perform their normal work or other corresponding work, deemed suitable for them considering their age, professional skills and other factors and providing a reasonable level of income, are entitled to the disability pension under the National Pensions Act. For those already 60 years of age, certain profession-specific alleviating factors are taken into consideration in the assessment. The permanently blind or immobile or persons in other situations of helplessness are always granted the permanent disability pension.

587. The national pension system also requires that rehabilitation potential of the person must be estimated before the decision on the pension is made. The disability pension under the National Pensions Act is granted for a determined or undetermined period of time, the former being in the form of the cash rehabilitation benefit. The temporary cash rehabilitation benefit is given for the period in which the person in question is deemed to remain unfit for work. The decision must always be accompanied by a therapy or rehabilitation plan.

588. The level of the national pension is determined in the law (EUR 628.85 a month for a single person and EUR 557.79 for both of a couple (year 2018)) and is adjusted annually through the national pension index. Other pensions reduce the sum of the national pension. The reduction takes place according to the principle that 50% of the aggregate of other pensions in excess of EUR 55.54 a month is deducted from the national pension (year 2018). In practice, this means that the other pensions reduce the national pension by 50% of their value until the entire national pension is deducted. The national pension can be defined as a 'pension-tested national pension'.

589. The survivors' pensions under the national pension system are different compared to the earning system pensions. As such, the basic provisions correspond to the employees' pension system in the sense that the surviving spouse who has or has had a child with the deceased and with the marriage contracted before the 65th birthday of the deceased is entitled to the pension. The major difference from the employee pensions system is the fact that the survivor pension is not paid to the surviving spouse who is already aged 65 or more.

590. The survivor's pension is paid as an initial pension or a continuing pension. The initial pension is payable to the survivor for six months after the death of the deceased. The initial pension is not payable to anyone after age 65 or if the survivor contracts a new matrimony before 50 years of age.

591. The survivor's right to the continuing pension depends on their own pension benefits. The continuing pension has a separate basic element and an earnings-related supplementary element. If the survivor receives the disability or old-age pension under the National Pensions Act, the continuing pension right does not exist. The survivor will be entitled to the continuing pension if the deceased and the survivor have a child under age 18 or the survivor shares the household with a child of age 18, either of the deceased or the survivor, and the child lived with them already at the time of death of the deceased.

592. The child's pension under the national pension is paid to the under-18-year-old child of the deceased. If the child is a full-time student, the time limit is 21 years. A full-orphan child can have the child's pension simultaneously after two deceased persons. The child will no longer be entitled to the child's pension if they receive the disability pension or survivor's pension under the National Pensions Act or similar benefit from abroad.

593. The national pension includes an initial pension and continuing pension payable to the surviving spouse. The initial pension is maximum EUR 324 per month (in 2018) and it is paid for six months. The initial pension is reduced by the national pension benefits received by the survivor as well as when the survivor becomes 65 or contracts new marriage under the age of 50 years.

594. Normally, the surviving spouse is not entitled to the continuing pension if a pension under the National Pensions Act is already paid. The deceased spouses and the survivor's child under 18 and an under-18-year-old child of either the survivor or the deceased provides the possibility to have the continuing pension.

595. The continuing pension is a fixed sum in euro per month, and the survivor's income and the time the deceased resided in Finland also have a bearing. The time lived in Finland plays a similar role for the survivor's pension as it would on the person's own pension. The continuing pension can be adjusted if the survivor's income changes, he or she contracts a new marriage or starts a live-in partnership or if the marriage or the partnership ends. The continuing pension will expire when the survivor becomes 65 years of age and also in cases where the survivors contracts new marriage under 50 years of age.

596. The child's pension under the national pension is paid to the under-18-year-old child. If the child is a full-time student, the time limit is 21 years. The child's pension is constituted by the basic element and the earnings-related supplementary element. The other pensions received by the child influence the supplementary element of the pension. Moreover, the time the deceased resided in Finland also impacts the child's pension amount.

597. Guarantee pension is a pension system maintained by the Kela, with the purpose of safeguarding the subsistence of a Finland-based pensioner by paying a pension out of State funds, if the pension otherwise is insufficient for reasonable subsistence. Pensioners living in Finland are eligible. The requirement of residence in Finland is at least three years after 16 years of age. Particular provisions apply to under-19-year-olds.

598. Persons receiving old-age pension are entitled to the guarantee pension. The same applies to those receiving a disability pension under the National Pensions Act or full disability pension under another Act. Moreover, the pension-like benefits under other statutory systems provide the right to the guarantee pension. Certain disabled persons may also receive the guarantee pension under exceptional grounds. The immigrants over 65 years of age, with no accrued pension, or a disabled person of 16 years of age is also eligible for the guarantee pension.

599. The full guarantee pension amounts to a sum defined in the law (EUR 775.27 in 2018). The guarantee pension is pension-tested in the sense that the national pension and other pensions as well as pension-like benefits will be deducted from it. Various discretional pension-like benefits paid either in Finland or abroad will also be deducted from the guarantee pension.

600. The guarantee pension will expire if the pensioner moves permanently or for a period over a year outside Finland or if the person no longer receives a pension or other benefit constituting the criterion of entitlement to the guarantee pension.

Part IX. People with a Handicap

Chapter 1. Social Integration

§1. General

601. The objective of disability care services is to improve and develop the capacities and functional conditions of the disabled persons so that they can lead as full and equal a life as possible, compared with those without a handicap. Disability must be seen as a relationship between the environment and the individual where the environment influences the individual's coping potential. However, here the discussion of 'disability care services' only refers to services and support measures while actions to impact the environment are not directly included in the realm of social welfare or disability care, even though they are connected with these issues.

602. 'Disabled person' refers to a person who, due to a disability or disease, has special long-term difficulties in coping with the usual everyday functions. According to the Services and Assistance for the Disabled Persons Act, the authorities must start to map out the service needs of the person in question within the seventh weekday from the date in which the authorities have been contacted for the purpose. Based on the information obtained, a service plan is drafted, followed by a decision on the measures no later than within three months from the application, unless the circumstances require otherwise.

603. Based on the Act in question, the general principle associated with societal development and aim to improve living conditions is that the authorities must promote and monitor the living conditions of the disabled persons, aiming to take measures to prevent the emergence of problems and eliminate difficulty. In fact, this extensive notion of the responsibilities covers all operations of the authorities. Specific services under the Services and Assistance for the Disabled Persons Act include rehabilitation instruction, adjustment training as well as other necessary services. The services can also be provided to close family members or caretakers of the disabled persons.

604. The disabled persons may be arranged day activities outside the home to promote their independent coping and social interaction. The disabled person can also receive personal assistance and financial aid. The financial aid may include a full or partial reimbursement of the costs incurred for the support measures that are necessary for the disabled as well as the extra expenses for clothing or special nutrition caused by the disability or disease. For aids, machines and devices required for daily coping, the reimbursement is half of their acquisition price while the conversion of standard machines and devices to meet the disabled person's needs is reimbursed fully.

605. The municipality must ensure that the services and support measures targeted at the disabled persons are organised, as far as the content and scope are concerned, in line with the needs existing in the municipality. Individual needs for assistance must be taken into account when the services are organised.

§2. Special Services for Persons with Severe Disabilities

606. Based on the Services and Assistance for the Disabled Persons Act, the persons in question have a subjective right to have certain services. First, they will have organised transportation services and related accompanying. In this context, the 'person with severe disabilities' is one with particular mobility difficulties who cannot use public transportation due to the injury or disease without encountering unreasonable difficulty. However, this provision is secondary in the sense that other statutory services are primary. Transportation and accompanying services are given for purposes such as work, study, running errands, societal participation, recreation and similar reasons. This means necessary transports are related to our daily life. Such transports include those within the individual's municipality or residence or to neighbouring municipalities. In addition to work and study-related transports, the individual must have every month at least eighteen one-way transport of daily life nature. This service may be subject to a fee corresponding to the public transportation ticket price.

607. In the organisation of day activities, 'person with severe disability' refers to an individual with a severe functional defect caused by a disability or disease who is not in the position to participate in exemplary employment and whose main income comes from the benefits paid on the basis of the disease or disability. As far as possible, the activities must be organised so that the person with the severe disability can attend five days a week, or less frequently in certain cases.

608. 'Personal assistance' refers to the indispensable help provided to the person with severe disability either at home or outside the home in daily functions, work and study, hobbies, societal participation or for the purpose of maintaining social contacts. The individuals with severe disabilities always and exclusively make their own choices regarding these activities. In this context, 'person with severe disability' is one who, due to a long-term or progressing disability or disease, absolutely and recurrently needs another person's help to cope with the above functions, and whose need for help is not mainly a result of diseases or functional defects associated with ageing. The particular problem with this provision is, in fact, to distinguish ageing from other disability. In organising the personal assistance, the opinion and wishes of the person with the severe disability must be taken into consideration. The assistance can be arranged by hiring a personal assistant, providing the person with service vouchers or by purchasing assistant services from public or private service providers.

609. Assisted living is one form of support provided for the persons with severe disabilities. Here, 'person with severe disabilities' is one who, due to the disability or disease, needs another person's help to cope with the daily functions permanently, in different times of the day or otherwise particularly amply.

610. The municipality must reimburse the expenses the person with severe disability has incurred for the changes in the apartment as well as the reasonable cost for aids and equipment acquired for the home if the person, due to the disability or disease, absolutely needs such aids and measures to cope with the functions of usual everyday life.

611. The disabled persons are entitled to interpretation services. The general purpose of the Act is to promote the disabled persons' possibilities to act as equal members of society. These operations are organised by the Social Insurance Institution Kela. The Act covers the visually impaired and those with a hearing or speech defect who need interpretation for their work, study, running errands, societal participation, hobbies or recreation. The frequency of the interpretation services is regulated so that the persons in question are entitled to receive a certain number of interpretation hours in a calendar year. If necessary, the limit can be exceeded. For a person involved in post-basic-education studies, the interpretation services must be organised to the degree needed by the student to manage the studies. Interpretation can also be organised abroad in which case the primary method is remote interpretation.

§3. Services for the Disabled Person under the Social Welfare Act

612. The services for the disabled persons are also provided under the Social Welfare Act. These services include the activities to support employability, rehabilitation and other support promoting the placement in work as well as the exemplary employment of the disabled persons.

613. In activities to support employability as well as rehabilitative and other operations to support work placements, the objective is to help persons who have particular long-term difficulties to cope with the work due to their disability, disease or other corresponding reason, with the ultimate aim of finding employment in the open labour market.

614. The 'exemplary employment of the disabled persons' means measures to maintain and promote their functional capacity. These activities are arranged for those who, due to their disability, are not in the position to participate in work under the employability-promoting activities and whose main income is based on social benefits.

§4. Services for the Mentally Disabled Person

615. Special care for the mentally disabled is given to persons whose development or mental functions have been prevented or disturbed due to a disease, defect or injury that is either inborn or has taken place during the development phase, and who cannot receive the necessary services under other legislation. The special care aims at promoting the person's coping with the daily functions, independent subsistence and adaptation to society as well as secure the necessary care and other caretaking.

616. The special care services include examinations with an extensive range of reports of various kinds, healthcare, necessary instruction, rehabilitation and functional coaching, organisation of exemplary employment and housing as well as corresponding operations that promote the adaptation to society. The persons can also be provided with personal aids and individual care and caretaking. Family members and other close persons can also receive instruction and advice as well as information about the special care services. The operations also include the prevention of developmental disturbances and other necessary measures.

617. To organise the special care, a specific plan is drafted and adopted for the person involved. This programme is considered binding to the authorities. It must be drafted in collaboration with the individual in question, their guardian or other person with the custody of the individual and the municipal social welfare authorities.

618. Special care can also be provided against the will of the person in question. This may be the case when the care cannot be organised otherwise and there is a reason to believe that, unattended, the individual's health or life could be at risk or that the behaviour and other factor show that the individual may put another person's safety at risk. In addition, the individual must be in immediate need of special care. The decision of committing the person to involuntary special care is based on an application made by the person who has custody of the mentally disabled person and in some cases by the municipal social welfare authorities. In certain respects, the legislation does not comply with the human rights requirements.

Chapter 2. Financial Allowances for the Handicapped

§1. Beneficiaries

619. The objective of the benefits to the disabled and chronically ill persons residing in Finland is to support their everyday coping, participation in employment and teaching as well as to maintain their functional capacity and possibilities to live at home, and to promote their rehabilitation and care. The benefits include the disability allowance paid to the under-16-year-olds and the allowance for the disabled persons over 16 as well as the basic-rate care allowance payable to the pensioners.

§2. Conditions

620. The benefits to the disabled persons are granted for an undetermined or fixed period of time. They are scaled according to the needs of the individual and may be the basic-rate, higher-rate or the highest rate allowance.

621. The general criterion for receiving these benefits is impaired functional capacity. It refers to the complication in the functions needed by the individual in everyday life due to the disease, defect or injury. Personal functions include mobility, dressing up, eating, nursing measures and personal hygiene functions and similar.

622. Children under age 16 are entitled to the disability allowance if the therapy, care and rehabilitation caused by the disease, defect or disability cause, during at least six months, greater burden and engagement than usual, compared with the same-age healthy child. The benefit takes the form of basic-rate disability allowance if the caretaker has this burden and engagement at least weekly. The higher-rate allowance is granted when the burden and caretaker's time-consuming engagement is daily while the highest rate allowance is applied if the burden and engagement is demanding and uninterrupted on a 24/7 basis.

623. Individuals over age 16 are entitled to the disability allowance if their functional capacity is deemed to have been impaired due to the disease, defect or disability uninterruptedly for at least a year. Moreover, the individual must be subject to inconvenience and need help, instruction and supervision or incur special expenses due to the disability, defect or disease.

624. The disability allowance for those over age 16 is granted as the basic-rate allowance if the disease or disability causes essential inconvenience and recurrent extra expenses. To receive the higher-rate disability allowance, the disease, defect or disability must cause significant inconvenience or the individual must need regular weekly help, instruction or supervision from another person to be able to function, or the disability must cause significant extra cost. The highest rate allowance may be paid to the severely disabled persons or those in need of daily, time-consuming help from another person in various personal functions or if the disability causes significant need for regular instruction and help or particularly sizeable extra costs.

625. Individuals over 16 years of age will be entitled to the basic-rate care allowance of pensioners if they are on a disability pension or old-age pension under the National Pensions Act or employee pension or disability pension under another pension-related Act. A person receiving benefits on the basis of occupational or traffic accidents may be entitled to the care allowance.

626. The estimated functional capacity must be uninterruptedly impaired due to disease, defect or disability for at least a year, or they must cause the need for help, instruction or supervision or extra costs.

627. The basic-rate allowance is available if the individual needs in the personal functions, household chores or errands outside the home, regular and at least weekly recurrent help, instruction or supervision by another person or the disability cause extra cost. The higher-rate care allowance is available to those who, in many of their personal functions, need time-consuming help by another person or who, due to their disability, need significant amount of regular instruction and supervision or extra costs. The condition for the highest rate care allowance is that the individual's need for care and supervision is uninterrupted or that the disability causes particularly high extra costs.

§3. Benefits

628. The basic-rate allowance payable to those under and over 16 years of age is EUR 92.14, the higher-rate allowance is EUR 215.87 and the highest rate allowance is EUR 416.91 per month in 2018. The basic-rate allowance of those on pension is EUR 70.52, the higher-rate allowance is EUR 153.63 and the highest rate allowance is EUR 324.85 a month in 2018.

Part X. Social Assistance

Chapter 1. Beneficiaries

629. The Constitution of Finland, the Charter of Fundamental Rights of the European Union and several human rights conventions require that State ensures the conditions for dignified human life and that government provides each individual with the necessary funds to this end. It is required that this benefit is secured as a subjective right. Both in principle and in practice the right applies to each person covered by the Finnish jurisdiction.

Chapter 2. Conditions

630. The general criterion for receiving social assistance is that the person in question is not able to independently provide for the security required for dignified human life. In practice, any and all other sources of income available to the person are first verified before income support is granted. This is also in compliance with the rights under the human rights conventions and Article 34:3 of the Charter of Fundamental Rights of the European Union.

631. Under the Income Support Act, social assistance is the lowest priority economic benefit. The purpose of the benefit is to ensure the subsistence for the person in question, with family, and to promote their independent coping. The secondary nature of social assistance is shown by the fact that the entitlement to social assistance can only come to exist if no income can be generated through work, self-employment, other benefits or the persons' own funds or income or through maintenance liability. All other means to generate income are taken into consideration before social assistance is granted. To receive social assistance, it is also required that the person in question – excluding children and those in retirement age – must be in active employment or work, receive unemployment benefits, be in institutional care or unable to accept work due to a disease or corresponding reason, or registered as an unemployed jobseeker. If this criterion is not met, the allowance may be lower.

Chapter 3. Amount of the Benefit

632. There are three forms of social assistance: basic social assistance, supplementary social assistance and preventive social assistance. In turn, basic social assistance is divided into the basic amount and other basic expenses. Each type has an independent purpose.

633. The basic amount included in the basic social assistance is used to cover the person's nutrition, clothing and minor healthcare expenses as well as those incurred for personal hygiene or home cleanliness, use of the local traffic, subscription to a newspaper, use of the telephone as well as hobbies and recreational activities as well as other expenses included in the daily subsistence of the person and the family. The basic amount is EUR 491.21 for a single person while the basic amount payable for a single parent is EUR 540.33 per month (in 2018). For spouses and partners, the allowance is smaller as well as for the over-18-year-old children living with the parents. The allowance for an underage child depends on the age and the number of other children in the family.

634. The basic amount can be reduced by the maximum of 20% for the above reasons and for the specific and verifiable refusal by the person to accept work that has been offered or about market measures that would ensure the income for a reasonably long period of time or if the person, through their own negligence, causes a situation where the authorities have not been able to offer work or such measures. The basic amount can be reduced by a maximum of 40% if the refusals are recurrent. The reduction only applies to the person in question but not to the family members. However, the minimum level of assistance is the security required by dignified human life. The other basic expenses with a bearing to the basic social assistance include the deductible under the Housing Allowance Act as well as certain other expenses.

635. When social assistance is granted, the income taken into consideration includes the available income of the person in question and the family, with certain exceptions. The exceptions include earnings and forms of assistance deemed minor, the regular income of a child under age 18 in excess of the child's own social assistance, the income needed for commuting, maternity grant and disability benefits. Moreover, 20% of the earned income is excluded from the income calculations, however, to the maximum of EUR 150 per month (in 2018). The purpose of the provision is to activate the recipient of the social allowance so that they can retain a part of the earned income without such sum reducing the amount of their social allowance.

636. In practice, the calculation for the social assistance is made by clarifying the family's income and available funds and if they are in excess of the basic amount of the family's basic social assistance, the basic amount cannot be paid. The practical calculation is relatively complex when assessment of income must also take the period of time and nature of the income into consideration.

637. When assessing the need for supplementary social assistance, particular expenses are taken into consideration, such as child day-care expenses, certain housing costs as well as expenses for independent coping related to the person's particular needs and circumstances, such as those incurred for a chronic disease or for the hobbies of the children. The supplementary social assistance is subject to the discretion of the authorities.

638. Preventive social assistance can also be granted. The objective is to promote the person's and the family's social security and independent coping. This form of assistance aims at preventing social exclusion and long-term dependency on social assistance. The objective may vary from activation to safeguarded housing or prevention of over-indebtedness.

Chapter 4. Claims and Administration

639. Social assistance is applied to Kela, the Social Insurance Institution. It can grant the basic social assistance and transfer the application for supplementary or preventive support to the municipality that takes the decisions in thesis cases.

Chapter 5. Reclaiming of Benefits Paid

640. Under the main rule, social assistance is not reclaimed. However, while granting social assistance, the authorities may decide that the assistance or part of it may be recovered if the recipient of the assistance has income or funds or entitlement to a benefit that secures their subsistence, not at their disposal at the moment of granting the assistance. In such cases, the social assistance can be granted for the waiting period and can be recovered retroactively form benefits granted later. Moreover, social assistance can be reclaimed from a person who wilfully provides erroneous information or neglects the duty of information.

Part XI. Claims and Adjudication

Chapter 1. Claims

§1. Introduction of Claims

641. Monetary benefits are applied for at the social security institution in charge of implementing the benefit in question. The Social Insurance Institution Kela is the competent authority in most cases. Kela's network of offices is quite extensive, and the applications for benefits can also be filed electronically and by mail. In view of the practical implementation of the health insurance, Kela has made direct reimbursement agreements with healthcare service providers. Under this model, the service users receive the Kela indemnity under the health insurance in the form of a reduction of the price paid to the service provider and the indemnity proper is paid to the service provider.

642. The pensions under the Pensions Acts are applied for at the office of the pension institution that is the latest insurer of the person in question. The employer chooses the insurance institution. Based on the agreement between the employee pension institutions and the Social Insurance Institution Kela, the latter receives applications addressed to any pension institution, forwarding them to the correct addressees. Correspondingly, the application for the pensions catered for by Kela can be submitted at the offices of the employee pension insurance institutions. The application form is the same throughout.

643. The procedure for unemployment protection is based on the obligation of the unemployed to register with the employment authorities as an unemployed jobseeker. Labour market support is applied for from Kela while the application for unemployment allowance is addressed either to Kela or the appropriate unemployment fund where the person in question is insured. The employment authorities will write an opinion whether the applicant meets the labour policy conditions and criteria, sending it to Kela or the unemployment fund that will grant the benefit. They are also the parties that determine whether the person in question is entitled to receive the benefit and how much the sum would be.

644. Social assistance is a benefit administered by Kela and municipalities. The benefit is primarily claimed from Kela which, if necessary, transfers the issue to the municipal social welfare authorities (*see* paragraph 639).

645. The claims for compensations under the Workers' Compensation Insurance Act are sent to the insurance company that has given the insurance. For farmers, the claims for compensation benefits are catered for by the Farmers' Social Insurance Institution.

646. Social welfare and healthcare services are sought from the municipality in question. Those wishing to benefit from the indemnities under the Health Insurance Act will seek the services offered by the private healthcare provider of their choice.

647. All public sector actors and private bodies administering public benefits must comply with the Administrative Procedures Act.

648. The major aspects related to the procedural duties and rights to be respected include the obligation to provide advice, the customer's right to be assisted by an attorney or other counsel or person, the right to have shortcomings in the documents rectified, attention to disqualification due to bias, right to speak for the incompetent person and the trustee's right to speak, various deadlines as well as the contents and motivations of the decisions.

649. Under the Administrative Procedures Act, the authorities have the duty of clarification. The obligation to provide clarifying information is divided between the interested person and the authorities so that the person in question must, if necessary, provide clarification for the grounds for the claims. Otherwise, it is the authorities' duty. Within the limitations covering the secrecy and confidentiality of the information involved, the authorities have the right to share information required in their work.

650. Normally, the persons concerned can express their opinion on this issue in the application but they must be heard in person if necessary. The hearing can be omitted only if it is obvious that there is no need to arrange for it.

651. The decision must be issued in writing in cases where the benefit relates to income security. At least negative decisions must be motivated. The decision must indicate the rights or obligations of the person in question or how the question has been otherwise solved.

652. Any appealable decisions on benefits must be accompanied by instructions for appeal with respective guidelines for proceeding in the case. If no appeal can be lodged against the decision, it must also be mentioned in the document. In certain cases, the appeal must be preceded by a complaint to the rectifying procedure within the administration, and the document of the decision must contain respective instructions.

653. Correspondingly, any decision on services must be accompanied with instructions of appeal or the rectifying process. The information must include the name of the competent authorities, period of appeal and complaint to rectify, the calculation of the said period and the authorities receiving the document of appeal or complaint.

654. The Administrative Procedures Act also contains provisions on how the decisions must be served to the interested person.

655. The various benefits related to income security are paid out to the banking accounts of the recipients. Cash payments can be made only in very exceptional cases. There is relatively abundant legislation covering the payments made to persons other than the one entitled to the benefits. The situations in question are those where the person is in institutional care or otherwise in public care.

656. The benefits and the related payments will discontinue when the underlying right no longer exists. For example, the beneficiary may find employment or the various age limits for allowance may be met, or the person's income undergoes a significant change. The legislation contains specific provisions on the situations where the benefits are revised and adjusted. The terms depend on the respective laws.

657. The benefits are paid no earlier from the date when the determined criteria are met. Payments may also be made retroactively for a period preceding the application. Recurrent payments are normally made monthly.

§2. Protection Against Seizure and Transfer

658. Income security benefits may be subject to recovery if they have been paid on unjustified grounds and to an excessive amount. In Finland, the same provisions on recovery are applied to various benefits, with the exception of certain differences that indispensably ensue from the nature of the benefit. Recovery can be foregone on equitable discretion or if the sum in question is minor. Renouncing recovery on equitable discretion may be possible on the condition that the unjustified payment of the benefit was not due to dishonest action by the recipient. Typically, equitable discretion is based on the recipient's circumstances and the potential impact of the recovery on the situation, the circumstances prevailing at the time of granting and paying the benefits as well as the time passed from the unjustified payment. The applicant's social and financial situation and potential maintenance obligation play a role.

659. Normally, a minor sum is a factor for renouncing recovery in a situation where the recovery process would be more costly than the sum in question.

660. If the unjustified payment of the benefit is based on a decision that was erroneous in origin, the decision must be rectified. A corresponding proposal for cancellation of the decision is submitted to the competent body of appeal.

661. In income security benefits, the first step of appeal is the rectification procedure. The objective of the process is to expedite the rectification of erroneous decision without prejudicing legal protection, thereby diminishing the number of cases at the appeal bodies, especially as concerns 'clear-cut cases' where the administrative instance agrees with the views of the appellant.

662. A complaint addressed to the Complaints Board or the Insurance Court is sent to the social security institution responsible for the decision. It may adjust the decision if it adopts all of the claims made in the complaint. If all claims are not adopted, the complaint must be subjected, within thirty days, to the appeal body, accompanied by the opinion of the authority that made the decision. If the social security institution approves part of the claims made, it can make an interim decision for that part.

663. The decision can be rectified in the interest of the applicant also in cases where the complaint has been lodged after the set deadline. In addition, the social security institution can always reopen the case, without the earlier decision preventing it from doing so, if the question at hand concerns the granting of a benefit earlier denied or the increase of a benefit previously granted. It is worth noting that new information and clarification can be obtained during the process, for example, on the state of health of the individual in question.

664. The social security institution can, with the consent of the person concerned, rectify its decision if it is based on clearly erroneous or incomplete information or obvious error in the application of the law. There are also provisions on corrections of obvious typos and miscalculations.

665. A decision on a social security benefit can be cancelled if it is based on erroneous or incomplete information or is patently against the law. The decision can be cancelled upon the request of the person concerned or the proposal by the organisation that made the decision. The most usual case of cancellation of a decision relates to proposals of the social security institution to recover benefits from the beneficiary to the detriment of the latter. The cancellation is normally based on new information presented in the case at hand.

666. Under the social security legislation, the benefits are only rarely protected against seizure. In practice, they are protected under Chapter 4 section 14 of the Enforcement according to which a benefit or compensation for expenses that has been granted for a specific purpose on the basis of pension or social welfare legislation may not be attached.

§3. LEGAL CAPACITY TO RECEIVE BENEFITS

667. Due to the personal character of social benefits, the individual is entitled to personally receive the benefit he or she has applied for. This also applies to situations where the benefit is paid to an under-aged person, such as the disability pension under the national pension scheme or the disability assistance payable to an individual over age 16.

668. Certain benefits, the housing allowance being the most important, are by nature payable to families. Correspondingly, income support is often paid to families as a whole even though the respective calculations are made for each family member separately. The reduction of income support always only applies to the person whose conduct is the cause of the measure.

669. With the consent of the beneficiary, certain benefits can be paid to another person. For example, the housing allowance can be paid directly to the landlord. The law prescribes that the private day-care allowance is paid directly to the facility organising the care.

Chapter 2. Adjudication

670. In issues concerning income security, the usual first instance of appeal is a body of a complaints board nature. These include Employee Pension Appeal Board, Accidents Appeal Board, Student Financial Aid Appeal Board and Social Security Appeal Board.

671. The Employee Pension Appeal Board examines complaints about decisions on employee pensions issues; correspondingly, the Accidents Appeal Board focuses on issues related to accident insurance, including occupational diseases, the Student Financial Aid Appeal Board on issues related to the financial aid to students and finally the Social Security Appeal Board on other issues, mostly decisions made by Kela and unemployment funds.

672. The Appeal Boards are not proper courts of law but by international standards, they could be classified as independent judicial bodies. They follow the court procedure and the Board members serve with the responsibility of a judge. Moreover, they are not subject to dismissal.

673. The supreme appellate body in the income security issues comprised of social security is the Insurance Court. It is the supreme judicial body to examine all appeals concerning the income security benefits under the social security system. The only exception is constituted by the accident insurance decisions made by the Insurance Court whereby the ultimate appeal can be addressed to the Supreme Court in certain questions related to claims for damages.

674. The appeals within the service system follow the general procedure under the administrative law. The appeals related to municipal services are made in line with the procedure generally applied to municipal decisions. In accordance, the applicant must first receive the decision with the associated claim for rectification. Based on this claim, the person in question can bring the case to a new discussion to the municipal board that took the first decision or, if the decision is made by a municipal official, to the appropriate municipal board. The Board must issue a written and motivated decision.

675. An appeal can be lodged against such a decision through a complaint addressed to one of the eight Administrative Courts in Finland. The Administrative Courts are general courts of law focusing on administrative law. Their rulings are further appealable, unless specifically prohibited. The Supreme Administrative Court is the ultimate court in issues of administrative law.

Selected Bibliography

Aarnio, Marko, Häkkinen, Olli, Jussila Niina, Järvinen, Pasi, Maisonlahti, Marjaana, Romo, Silja ja Sollo, Anneli: Työttömyysturva. Edita Publishing Oy, Helsinki 2003.

Aerschot, Paul Van: Köyhät ja laki: toimeentulotukilainsäädännön kehitys oikeudellistumisprosessien valossa. Suomalainen lakimiesyhdistys, 1996.

Arajärvi, Pentti: Johdatus sosiaalioikeuteen. Talentum, Helsinki 2011.

Arajärvi, Pentti: Toimeentuloturvan oikeellisuus. Toimeentuloturvaa koskevan lainsäädännön suhde perustuslakiin, erityisesti perusoikeuksiin, ihmisoikeuksiin ja yhteisöoikeuteen. Kela Sosiaali- ja terveysturvan tutkimuksia 68. Helsinki 2002.

Avuttomuus lainsäädännössä. Sosiaali- ja terveydenhuollon ulkopuoliset tekijät -työryhmä. Raportti I. Sosiaali- ja terveysalan tutkimus- ja kehittämiskeskus, Helsinki 2008.

Hagfors, Robert, Hellsten, Katri ja Sakslin, Maija (toim.): Suomen kansan eläke. Kelan tutkimusosasto, Vammala 200885.

Hellsten, Katri: Vaivaishoidosta hyvinvointivaltion kriisiin, Helsinki 1993.

Hellsten, Katri, Hidén, Mikael ja Sakslin, Maija (toim.): Sosiaaliset oikeudet ja sosiaaliturva. Kela. Sosiaali- ja terveysturvan katsauksia 48. Helsinki 2001.

Huhtanen, Raija: Mitä tarkoitetaan sosiaalisten oikeuksien yksilökohtaisuudella? Julkaisussa Aerschot, Ilveskivi ja Piispanen (toim.): Juhlakirja Kaarlo Tuori 50 vuotta. Helsingin yliopiston julkisoikeuden laitos, Helsinki 1998, s. 171–185.

Huhtanen, Raija: Toimeentulotuen myöntäminen. Julkisoikeudellinen tutkimus hallinto- ja hallintolainkäyttöviranomaisen soveltamiskäytännöstä. Jyväskylä 1994.

Hytti, Helka: The Finnish Employment and Income Security Models in a Nordic Comparison. Kela, Social Security and Health Research: Working Papers 52/2006. Helsinki 2006.

Johanson, Jan-Erik, Lassila, Jukka ja Niemelä, Heikki (toim.): Eläkevalta Suomessa. Taloustieto Oy, Helsinki 2011

Korpiluoma, Riitta, Grönlund, Harri, Herrlin, Ove, Kekäläinen, Jaana, Kouvonen, Keijo, Levander, Minna, Lilius, Sonja, Mustonen, Pasi, Määttä, Mikko, Perälehto-Virkkala, Anne, Takanen, Maijaliisa, Tuomikoski, Jaakko: Työeläke. Bookwell Oy, Porvoo 2011.

Mattila, Yrjö (toim.): Toimeentuloturva. Finanssi- ja vakuutuskustannus Oy, Helsinki 2017.

Mikkola, Matti: Social Human Rights of Europe. Karelactio, Porvoo 2010.

Selected Bibliography

Mikkola, Matti, Pietiläinen, Seppo ja Valpola, Olli: Suomalainen toimeentuloturva. Karelactio, Helsinki 2002.

Tällä lailla sosiaaliturvaa. Sosiaaliturvan saamisedellytyksistä ja -takeista. Hyvinvointivaltion rajat -hanke. Sosiaali- ja terveysalan tutkimus- ja kehittämiskeskus, Helsinki 2006.

Tuori, Kaarlo – Kotkas, Toomas: Sosiaalioikeus. WSOYpro, Juva 2008.

Index

The numbers here refer to paragraph numbers.

Accident, accident insurance, 23, 30, 52, 102, 144, 377–414, 527, 559, 625, 645, 670–673
Adoption, 283, 288, 337, 345, 358, 368–370, 373–375
Åland, 14, 502

Basic rights, 12, 37, 62–65, 73, 75, 96, 347
Basic-rate care allowance, 408, 492, 619, 625–628

Child benefit, 34, 284–286, 452
Child home care allowance, 55, 303–310, 320–323, 353
Child welfare, 33, 47, 59, 92, 149, 265, 316, 318
Childcare leave, 301–308
Civil and political rights, 12, 37
Constitution, 10–13, 37, 62, 65–77, 79, 96, 146, 319, 347, 629
Council of Europe, 16, 17, 37
Court, 80, 81, 85, 86, 197, 210, 212, 213, 287, 318, 662, 672–675

Day care, 35, 55, 155, 197, 257, 264, 294–300, 303, 304, 311, 312, 637
Disabled person, disability, incapacity to work, 23, 46, 47, 54, 56, 66, 91, 92, 255, 264, 267, 306, 325, 327–377, 393, 399, 400, 405, 408–411, 442, 450, 452, 491, 520–525, 541, 543, 557–581, 586, 587, 591, 592, 598, 601–628, 635, 667

Early childhood education, 294–300, 303
Economic, social and cultural rights, 12, 37, 62–65, 73, 82
Education, training, 15, 22, 35, 37, 50, 52, 72, 103, 108, 185–187, 202, 274–277, 391, 398, 418–427, 431, 435, 446, 464, 465, 473, 478–484, 563, 569, 571
Employee, 52, 105–134, 188–190, 301–308, 314, 315, 334, 335, 339–344, 363, 378–381, 385, 387–391, 412–414, 455, 459, 476, 485–489, 499–539, 558–561, 565, 569, 576, 580
Employee pension, 23, 35, 44, 52, 82, 99–103, 106, 111, 114, 118, 121, 122, 127, 130–133, 450, 492–580, 589, 642, 670, 671
Employer, 34, 52, 99, 106–121, 125–134, 144, 158, 188–190, 266, 302, 305, 307, 308, 310, 313, 334, 335, 340–344, 354, 364, 367, 372, 378, 379, 387–389, 391, 407, 412, 413, 420, 440, 459, 486, 500, 503–506, 642
Employment, 21, 38, 42, 43, 71, 155, 415–490, 512–614, 656
Employment services, 145, 415–423, 446
Entrepreneur, 359, 363, 381, 423, 456, 457, 460, 472, 503, 504, 508, 547, 549
Equality, 37, 38, 42, 54, 73, 164, 176, 255, 319, 416, 439, 601, 611
European Union, 16, 17, 19, 23, 24, 57, 65, 74, 111, 174, 270, 271, 378, 379, 500, 345, 505, 511, 555, 629, 630

Farmer, 100, 102, 135–143, 160, 359, 384, 460, 502, 513, 547–556, 645
Finnish, (language) 3, 35, 299, 435
Finnish Centre for Pensions, 101, 106, 123, 506, 507, 546
Funeral benefit, 330

Government transfers to municipalities, see state subsidy
Guarantee pension, 492, 581, 597–600

Index

Handicap, handicapped, 262, 377, 410, 450–452, 601–628
Healthcare, 15, 23, 32, 35, 40, 43, 46–50, 61, 67, 76, 83, 90, 92, 94, 98, 145–149, 153, 162–204, 233, 234, 238–269, 344, 641, 646
Healthcare professional, 162, 173, 174, 273–280, 386
Healthcare services, see Social and healthcare services
Health insurance, 23, 35, 52, 66, 91, 97, 109, 113, 116, 120, 126, 134, 137, 143, 154, 159, 163, 175, 199, 234, 339, 341, 347, 450, 566, 567, 641, 646
Housing allowance, 59, 91, 452, 492, 634, 668, 669
Human rights, Fundamental rights, 17, 37, 65, 74, 219, 618, 629, 630

Immigration, immigrant integration, 8, 433–439
Incapacity to work, see disable person
Income divide, 37, 43, 54
Income security, income protection, 41, 45, 57, 81, 83, 86, 91, 99, 104, 105, 491, 492, 651, 655, 658, 661, 670, 673
Insurance Court, 81, 86, 662, 673
Interpretation, 80, 411, 611
Intoxicant abusers, 47, 48, 167, 187, 220

Kela, see National Insurance Institution

Labour market support, 91, 107, 158, 427–429, 438, 444–484, 643
Labour training, 424–426, 481–484

Maternity package and grant, 283, 635
Means testing, 53, 468
Mental health, 48, 167, 187, 205–220, 264
Mentally disabled, 264, 615–618
Municipality, federation of municipalities, 15, 29, 36, 38, 60, 61, 76, 80, 88, 93–95, 97, 98, 105, 146–156, 163, 167–174, 183–203, 239, 249, 250, 260, 268, 269, 298–300, 303, 304, 310, 312, 392, 430, 434, 437, 439, 502, 509, 605, 610, 618, 639, 644, 646, 674

National Insurance Institution, Kela, 80, 83, 85, 86, 91, 97, 129, 154, 155, 234, 236, 238, 242, 245, 288, 289, 326, 447, 502, 597, 611, 639, 641–644, 671
National pension, 33, 35, 44, 56, 291, 450, 492–495, 581–600, 625, 667

Occupational diseases, 23, 144, 377–414, 671
Occupational healthcare, 83, 110, 167, 188–190, 260, 266, 267, 334
Old age, 66, 491, 492, 498, 581–600
Old-age pension, 191, 396, 451, 492, 493, 494, 497, 499–535, 543, 545–555, 557, 568, 570, 575, 576, 583, 591, 598, 625
Outpatient care, 201, 260–262

Parental allowance, parental leave, 45, 52, 159, 301–308, 310, 321, 338–345, 354–359, 368–376, 451, 527
Parental insurance, 23, 91, 137, 154
Paternity allowance, paternity leave, 339, 342, 354, 368, 369, 374, 376
Patient, 48, 97, 164, 165, 171–182, 200–219, 221, 233–242, 259–267, 271, 276, 277, 386, 392
Patient ombudsman, 182, 219
Pension institute, institution, 99–102, 106, 123, 127, 141, 506–509, 558, 562, 569, 642–645
Pre-primary education, 298, 312, 324
Public service, 39, 67, 233, 415, 416, 608

Reclaiming, 640, 658–666
Rehabilitation, 52, 54, 91, 109, 110, 162, 167, 176, 193, 200, 201, 205, 219, 221, 238, 242, 264, 267, 329, 336, 337, 362, 393, 394, 399, 400, 407, 418, 431, 457, 491, 527, 557–580, 587, 603, 612, 613, 616, 619, 622
Renewed European Social Charter, 65
Residence basis of the social security system, 23, 58

Self-employed, 99, 103, 105, 110, 116, 120, 126, 135–143, 160, 188, 297, 309, 332, 335, 359, 363, 381, 383, 425, 456, 457, 460, 462, 464, 471, 472, 485, 494, 495, 502–504, 508, 513, 518, 545–556, 581, 631
Sickness allowance, 110, 199, 327–364, 450, 527
Social allowance, 23–25, 53, 91, 107, 154, 347, 635
Social and healthcare services, 15, 17, 23, 40, 43, 46–50, 57, 58, 67, 83, 88, 90, 92,

94, 145–148, 153, 220, 248–269, 334, 431, 601–618
Social assistance (minimum income), 23–25, 53, 91, 107, 154, 426–429, 437, 438, 452, 635
Social assistance (last-resort support for subsistence), 34, 53, 427–429, 437, 438, 452, 629–640, 644
Social benefit, 36, 59, 348, 362, 451, 452, 614, 667
State subsidy, government transfers to municipalities, 76, 83, 145–153, 233
Social insurance, 23, 30, 33, 52, 87, 126, 161, 414
Study, studying, 49, 72, 83, 157, 186, 187, 297, 316, 362, 363, 368, 384, 401, 405, 424–426, 471, 472, 478, 488, 528, 592, 596, 606, 608, 611
Subjective right, 65, 173, 297, 421, 606, 629
Survivors' pension, 35, 59, 403, 493, 494, 536–544, 556, 582, 589–596
Swedish language, 3, 10, 299, 435

Tax, taxation, 3, 15, 24, 26, 36, 37, 39, 40, 42, 51, 56, 76, 104, 105, 118, 120, 128, 129, 139, 143, 145–161, 233, 283, 293, 300, 349, 350, 359, 459, 495
Training, see education

Unemployment, unemployment security, unemployment benefit, unemployed, 21–23, 33, 35–37, 45, 52, 66, 82, 91, 103, 107, 108, 112, 115, 119, 121, 123, 128, 133, 137, 142, 149, 151, 155, 158, 321, 325, 347, 362, 363, 415–490, 527, 631, 643, 670
Unemployment fund, 5, 22, 33, 103, 115, 119, 128, 142, 155, 350, 444, 447, 456, 460, 643, 671
Unemployment Insurance Fund, 103, 123, 128, 155
United Nations, 16, 17, 318
Universality, 39–41, 53, 57, 94

Index

Made in the USA
Monee, IL
13 September 2026

62974268R00096